MEET THE SAINTS

Cover and book design by Mark Sullivan
Cover image © Jozef Sedmak | Dreamstime.com

LIBRARY OF CONGRESS CATALOGING-IN-PUBLICATION DATA
Meet the saints / introduction by Robert Morneau.
p. cm.
Includes bibliographical references.
ISBN 978-1-61636-002-3 (alk. paper)
1. Christian saints. I. Morneau, Robert F., 1938-
BX4655.3.M44 2011
270.092′2—dc22
2011005937

ISBN 978-1-61636-002-3

Published by St. Anthony Messenger Press
28 W. Liberty St.
Cincinnati, OH 45202
www.AmericanCatholic.org
www.SAMPBooks.org

Printed in the United States of America.
Printed on acid-free paper.

11 12 13 14 15 5 4 3 2 1

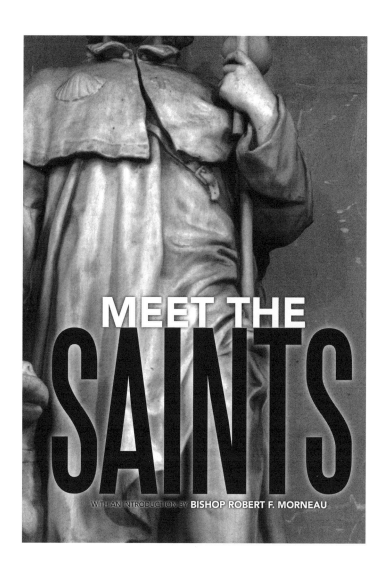

MEET THE
SAINTS

WITH AN INTRODUCTION BY **BISHOP ROBERT F. MORNEAU**

ST. ANTHONY MESSENGER PRESS
Cincinnati, Ohio

| CONTENTS |

v

ABOUT THIS BOOK

Originally published as a twelve-month newsletter series, "Walking With the Saints," this book brings together an introduction of saints from across the centuries and around the world. With contributions from popular authors such as William H. Shannon, Robert F. Morneau, Joanne Turpin, Albert Haase, Mitch Finley, Kathy Finley, Vicky Hébert, Denis Sabourin, Anthony J. Salim, and Mary Cummins Wlodarski, each chapter tells the story of some of our church's most famous saints.

In addition to learning something about the historical context in which these holy men and women lived their lives, you'll also find answers to some frequently asked questions and be invited to "step out in faith" by following the examples of the saints.

For more information on some of the saints in this book, check out the bibliography for additional recommended reading.

| INTRODUCTION |

A teacher from many years ago forever changed my concept of what a saint is. Fr. Gordon Gilsdorf, in his book *The Same Five Notes* wrote this poem entitled "A Saint."

> We look
> for mystic gold
> and silvered ecstasy
> and find a tempered, twisted piece
> of steel.[1]

At the age of ninety-nine, John Wooden, the famous basketball coach from UCLA and holder of ten national championships, co-authored a book, *A Game Plan for Life: The Power of Mentoring.* Coach Wooden spoke about seven mentors in his life (two of whom were Abraham Lincoln and Blessed Mother Teresa of Calcutta) and of seven people he mentored. Wooden reaffirmed the tremendous importance of having teachers and models on our life's journey.

The saints have been, throughout the ages, teachers and witnesses of gospel living. These holy women and men are held up by the church as examples of what discipleship is all about. They followed Jesus and lived the life of the Holy Spirit in powerful ways, sometimes in the public arena, as in the life of St. Thomas More, sometimes in a hidden cloister like St. Thérèse of Lisieux. Some saints were scholars or kings, some were housewives and mystics, some were farmers and fishermen. Regardless of their state in life, they all heard God's call and responded fully in love and fidelity.

Lest we put our beloved saints on an unreachable pedestal, we know from their own writings and confessions that they, like all of us, were also sinners. We need but read the *Confessions of St. Augustine* to witness the struggles of a fellow pilgrim who contended with unbridled sensuality, intellectual arrogance, and blatant deception. We know from the Gospels the story of Peter's denial of the Lord and of St. Paul's persecution of the early church. Saints were flawed individuals who, through God's mercy and grace, were able to embrace God's forgiveness and become transmitters of God's extravagant love and mercy. It is not surprising that humility, living in the truth of things, was foundational to their lives.

One of the articles of our faith is that we believe in the communion of saints. Right now, at this very moment, the saints in heaven intercede for us. Where they have gone, we hope to follow. In eternity this church triumphant continues to be with us in powerful ways—through prayer, the example of their lives, the legacy of their writings. On the Feast of All Saints, November 1, we gather in worship to honor the women and men who said yes to that narrow, royal road of obedience and love. The following poem I wrote speaks of the great doctrine of the communion of saints:

Communion of Saints
A mighty band of brothers and sisters,
a great cloud of witnesses,
the society we call the communion of saints.
Through them God's radiance shines,
in them the poison of self-interest is killed,
from them we receive support still.
Living and real they are,
still doing good, now from heaven.
Intimates of God,
His friends and, yes, warriors.

Think of them, love them, learn from them.
We and they are one society,
the Church visible and invisible,
one family consecrated to God's will.

Do saints have any relevance to our contemporary age, a culture so pragmatic, active, and frenetic? Are not our true mentors and models individuals who excel in the fields of science, politics, economics, sports, and cultural affairs? Simply put: Who are our heroes, or do we have any at all?

Saints, canonized and uncanonized, are significant to our times for three reasons. First, they lived authentic human lives. They walked the path, not of fame or fortune or power, but the way of love, compassion, and forgiveness. The saints embraced the paschal mystery of dying to self and rising to new life in Jesus. They walked to and through the cross into the mystery of the resurrection.

Second, the saints challenge our potential and disturb our complacency. Reading a book such as Robert Ellsberg's *All Saints: Daily Reflections on Saints, Prophets, and Witnesses for Our Time* stretches us as we see so many great people respond so generously to the gifts that God gave them. In reading the lives of the saints we are often convicted of our selfishness and greed, our self-indulgence and pride. The saints were stewards of God's gifts and made a contribution to the common good and the Kingdom of God. They were truly instruments and ambassadors of God's grace.

A third reason why saints are relevant today is that they put first things first. This sense of priority is desperately needed in our times. The options are so many, the voices calling us here and there so distracting, the rapidity of change and constant mobility so overwhelming. The saints had a center. They knew the one thing necessary, that *unum necessarium*. God was first in their lives, and everything and everyone else revolved around that center. The saints had that unique and beautiful habit of referring everything to that center, that still point of life. Such a way of life offers that possibility of peace and joy.

We might turn to a third-grader to appreciate the relevancy of saints, in another poem I wrote:

A Saint
A third-grader got it right:
"A saint is someone that
the light shines through."

She was looking at a stained-glass window—
the one St. Francis inhabits.
Every morning the light comes
and St. Francis lets it pass through.

Saints are bearers of light
and love
and life.
Just ask any third-grader.[2]

Meet the Saints can be used in several ways. It can be a source of personal prayer, taking one chapter a month and spending ten to fifteen minutes pondering the life and the work of a particular saint. At the end of the year, nearly forty saints will have enriched our list of mentors and models. Or, after reading a chapter, you might run off to the library or search the Internet to get a more comprehensive work on the life of that saint, be it a biography or autobiography. Third, during the season of Advent or Lent, this book might serve as one's primary resource for spiritual reading.

Another use of this volume is of a social nature. By gathering some friends or members of one's faith community, a schedule of twelve weeks could be set up and at each meeting a discussion of a chapter could be held. By sharing insights and observations, we will grow together toward that spiritual maturity that St. Paul so treasured.

Finally, *Meet the Saints* offers the possibility of developing a precious friendship with one or another of the saints herein. This experience will be life transforming, for friendship is one of the greatest gifts in the entire world. In fact, St. Thomas Aquinas describes grace as *amacitia Dei*, friendship with God. That is the heart of sanctity.

Sainthood

They should, these saints,
these heavenly hall of famers,
inspire and strengthen us struggling pilgrims
as we journey toward the city of God.
Why then am I irritated by their goodness?
Why then am I disturbed by their setting the bar so high?
Is it jealousy
or an awareness of how unloving I am?

One of my five siblings
was identified as our mother's helper,
as one whose room was always clean and orderly,
yes, as one who was courteous and kind.
Trouble for the rest of us—
a saint in our home.

So, do saints inspire and strengthen,
or do they irritate and disturb?
Perhaps, on any given day,
in the various seasons of life,
they do both.

Their glory, their light, their love
have many holy functions.

Most Reverend Robert F. Morneau
Auxiliary Bishop of Green Bay
September 22, 2010

| CHAPTER ONE |

Women Who Knew Jesus

Joanne Turpin

Some of the first holy people we honor as heroes and saints of our church lived alongside Jesus. We all know of the twelve apostles, but Jesus counted women among his friends and disciples as well. In a society that viewed females as "inferior in all things" (so bluntly put by a first-century Jewish historian), Jesus' ways were shocking indeed. He acted as if the many restrictions placed on women simply did not exist. Such restrictions prevented them from aspiring to any meaningful role in religious life—the two primary ones being Temple priests and scribes. When Jesus offered women the chance to be part of his ministry, they responded with an eagerness that suggested they'd been waiting for just this moment in time.

SALOME, MOTHER OF JAMES AND JOHN
Feast day: June 29

When life is going well, there's little reason to change. That is surely what Zebedee thought, for he had a prosperous fishing business, the help of his two sons, and a wife to manage the household and mend nets or sails as needed. It must have been like cold water dashed in his face when James and John abandoned the family business to become followers of an itinerant teacher named Jesus.

1

Whether the idea originated with Zebedee or whether Salome took it upon herself to keep a close eye on their sons, she appears early, along with other women, traveling openly in the company of Jesus' disciples. Society would have looked askance at such behavior. One can imagine the women being ridiculed or shunned, even by friends and neighbors.

Though the women in Jesus' company came from a mix of backgrounds—one had included a member of Herod Antipas's royal court—Salome had something in common with at least one other: Mary of Cleopas. Mary's son James was also one of the twelve apostles.

Mother and Disciple
Judging from the nickname Jesus gave Salome's high-spirited James and John, "Sons of Thunder," she must have had her hands full. Her sons (along with Peter) comprised Jesus' inner circle. This distinction may have gone to their heads. Along the road to Jerusalem, with Salome present, they request the most prominent places in the Kingdom. Jesus tells them they have failed to understand his words about the necessity of the cross. But they would learn. (In AD 44, James was martyred.)

In the meantime, Salome and the other women minister to the throngs that gather to hear Jesus speak and to seek his healing. It would have been a matter of transferring skills acquired at home to a larger setting. Caring for the family's sick, for example, was women's customary role. Now, in marketplaces and open plains, they assist the lame, the blind, and the sick who await their turn to be healed.

And when Jesus teaches the multitudes on hillside or lakeshore, the elderly require help and mothers with young children need looking after. To get a sense of the immensity of the undertaking, we read Matthew's account of the miraculous feeding of five thousand men in which he adds "not counting the women and children."

Faithful to the End
But the halcyon days of adoring crowds near an end as Jesus faces growing hostility from religious authorities outraged at his teachings. Plotting against him begins. Once set in motion, events move swiftly. After a sham trial, the Roman governor hands Jesus over to soldiers who march him through the streets of Jerusalem to Calvary.

Though Jesus is abandoned by almost everyone who had claimed to be his follower, his female disciples—Salome among them—stand fast. By their presence at the cross, they identify themselves with a convicted criminal, an enemy of the state. It's risky business, for the mob surrounding them is in an ugly mood, jeering and cheering as Jesus is nailed to the cross. Surely though, worst of all, the women experience that feeling of utter helplessness as they watch a loved one suffer unbearable pain.

Late in the afternoon, Jesus draws his last breath and is taken down from the cross. Our final picture of Salome shows her and other grief-stricken women going to the tomb on Easter morning. Without a doubt, she later returned home to Galilee, to further Jesus' mission there.

MARTHA AND MARY OF BETHANY
Feast day: June 4
In today's world, theirs would be called a nontraditional household: Martha and Mary and their brother, Lazarus, all single adults. When Luke's Gospel introduces us to the two sisters at home, Jesus is there, in a scene that suggests a close friendship. It is a picture of domesticity: Martha preparing a meal for their guest, Mary sitting at Jesus' feet and absorbed in his words. But a first-century Jewish onlooker would find this a disturbing—even shocking—scene, for women must never entertain a male guest without a kinsman present, and Lazarus is nowhere in sight.

When Martha expresses her frustration to Jesus, it is not so much that Mary is failing to help her. Rather, she sees her sister sitting in the traditional posture of a disciple. A female might, in rare instances, receive some religious instruction, but only from a father or husband. Disregarding the prevailing view, Jesus tells Martha that it is a matter of choice: She can choose to do the same as Mary. (A later incident shows that Martha accepts the invitation to deepen her faith.)

A Place Apart, a Stunning Miracle
Whenever Jesus comes to Jerusalem, he finds a ready welcome in Bethany, a quiet village on the Mount of Olives, about a half-hour walk to the holy city. After a day of teaching and healing, Jesus needs a place apart to restore his spirits. In Galilee, he has only to go up into the nearby hills. But in hectic, crowded Jerusalem, it isn't until he becomes acquainted with the family in Bethany that he finds his sanctuary.

In his last months, Jesus spends his most prolonged period of teaching daily in the Temple. When attempts to arrest him begin, he withdraws for a time to the Jordan River Valley. There he receives the sisters' message that Lazarus is critically ill, but Jesus fails to arrive before Lazarus dies.

Upon hearing that at last Jesus is approaching, Martha rushes out to greet him, heedless of the custom that the immediate family leaves the house only to go to the tomb. (The closer to the holy city and the higher the social status, the more stringently rules are applied. Lazarus's tomb is that of a wealthy person.) In the ensuing conversation, Martha makes a public declaration of faith, proclaiming Jesus as the Messiah. After that, Jesus performs his greatest miracle—the raising of Lazarus.

Oblation and Refuge
We see the family for the last time at a banquet in a neighbor's house. Not surprisingly, Martha is serving. In Jewish culture, except for the Passover Supper, banquets were male-only affairs.

Yet Mary enters the dining room, bringing an alabaster jar of a costly, fragrant ointment. What she does next leaves the disciples momentarily speechless. She breaks the jar to pour its precious contents over Jesus' feet. To wipe up the excess, Mary unbinds her hair—something never allowed in the presence of men. When they begin complaining about the wastefulness, Jesus commends her for her beautiful deed.

In subsequent centuries, ignorant of the revolutionary actions of the sisters, Martha is commonly named a patroness of cooks. In scholarly confusion over the different Marys in the Gospel, Mary of Bethany's identity got lost in the Western Church, though the Eastern Orthodox Church long ago assigned her a feast day. Perhaps the sisters should best be remembered for the refuge they provided for Jesus, even when he was a hunted man.

Mary Magdalene
Feast day: July 22

The character of Mary Magdalene, as commonly portrayed in books, theater, film and art, is more fiction than fact. How this "apostle to the apostles" came to be regarded as a reformed prostitute is owed to a sixth-century pope. He equated the "seven demons" Mary was healed of with the seven capital sins (a new theology in his time), lust being the worst. The pope's homilies received wide circulation, capturing the popular imagination, and the label stuck. Only in recent decades has a concerted attempt been made to set the record straight.

The Gospel story of Mary Magdalene begins with her leadership of a band of women who, according to Luke, formed part of Jesus' company of disciples. Jesus had cured her of "seven demons"—denoting the severity of an illness mystifying to doctors. Her health restored, she committed her life and all she possessed to supporting Jesus' ministry.

An Exceptional Woman

Mary's wealth was probably derived from either an inheritance or business. Being identified by her town, Magdala, rather than relationship to a spouse or male kinsman, tells us that Mary was a never-married daughter who consequently became independent in the eyes of the law. As such, she could engage in business so long as a male guardian handled legal matters. Magdala, by the Sea of Galilee, was a thriving hub for fishing and boat-building.

Mary Magdalene's name is found fourteen times in Gospel passages—more than many of the male apostles. Her prominence is further suggested by the placement of her name whenever others are mentioned. She heads the list with one exception: when she stands at the foot of the cross with Jesus' mother.

Though she was never known to waver in her support of Jesus, Mary Magdalene's actions in Jesus' final days best exemplify her unflinching commitment. Through the agonizing hours of his crucifixion and the desolate Sabbath that followed, she holds her band together. At dawn on Sunday morning, she leads them once again. This time, it is to perform the last service they can offer for their beloved Master: a reverential anointing.

To their dismay, they find the tomb empty and think that either Roman soldiers or local authorities removed the body. When her companions leave, Mary hurries to tell Peter and John the distressing news. They return with her, look into the tomb, also fail to understand and then depart. A heartbroken Mary, however, lingers near the tomb.

Bearer of Good News

Nothing could have prepared her for what happened next. Jesus appears at her side and speaks her name. "Teacher!" she cries. Overcome with joy, she would have wished time to stand still. But Jesus has work for her, commissioning her to go tell his brothers the Good News of the Resurrection.

When she runs to where the men are hiding and exclaims, "I have seen the Lord!" they dismiss her words. (Jesus would later reprimand them for their lack of faith.) Because of her faithfulness, Mary Magdalene becomes the bearer of the message that remains at the heart of Christian belief.

Tradition has Mary accompanying the apostle John and Jesus' mother to Ephesus, in Asia Minor (modern Turkey), where she spent the rest of her life. The memory of Mary Magdalene's discipleship is preserved in writings of the church Fathers from the early centuries. Even theologians who expressed a low opinion of women (one calling them "the devil's gateway") heaped nothing but praise on Mary Magdalene. Their favorite title for her: the apostle to the apostles.

STEPPING OUT IN FAITH

Take advantage of opportunities to do good. Follow in the footsteps of…

- Salome, who transferred her skills as wife and mother to minister to the crowds that followed Jesus. Consider sharing your talents, abilities and knowledge in new ways within a parish ministry or social outreach effort.
- Martha and Mary of Bethany, who provided Jesus with the support of friendship and a refuge, a place apart. Invite your pastor or member of your parish staff to dinner or for coffee. Write a note to thank a minister for his or her efforts on your community's behalf.
- Mary Magdalene, who committed her life and possessions to Jesus and carried the news of the Resurrection to the apostles. Commit to more fully living your faith in Jesus and the promise of the Resurrection. What will that look like in your life?

| CHAPTER TWO |

Saints of the Eastern Traditions

Fr. Anthony J. Salim

When most people hear the term *Catholic*, chances are good they first think of the Roman Catholic tradition. However, those who know of the church's foundations outside Jerusalem realize that the culture of the earliest church changed rapidly. Within the Roman Empire, the gospel message took on the look and feel of local cultures. Today we speak of the gospel being "inculturated."

These differences in traditions—and the rich ways the faith was proclaimed, explained, expressed, lived, and celebrated in worship and prayer—remain with us today. Within the universal Catholic communion of churches are those called "Eastern Churches." They remain close to the Eastern origins of Christianity in style and character.

ST. EPHREM *(c. 306–373)*
Feast day: July 9

"Praise God!" the young woman said to Deacon Ephrem as they exited the main doors of their parish church. "The new verses you have written for Our Lady on her feast day are wonderful! They made me think of how good our God is to us in Jesus and how lucky we are to be able to worship today."

"Thank you, child," Ephrem replied. "I am still amazed at how God allows me to compose music for the church, and how you and your choir members can learn the verses so quickly. Our Aboon [Pastor] seemed pleased as well."

Life for Christians in the land between the great rivers—the Tigris and the Euphrates—sometimes had these nice moments in it. But as a pawn in wars between the two great empires—the Roman and the Persian—Mesopotamia felt the tensions of an unstable political situation. The people of Ephrem's time knew what it was to suffer at the hands of the great rulers who fought for control over this important place.

All Must Eat

Ephrem's Syrian communities in Nisibis and Edessa knew ravages to their homeland from nature as well. Although situated in the fertile crescent, this land was prone to earthquakes and, at times, famine—events that take their toll on the lives of people.

After an earthquake devastated Edessa, Ephrem made his way to the point designated for the distribution of food. Tradition tells us that during the famine that hit Edessa in 372, Ephrem was horrified to learn that some citizens were hoarding food. When he confronted them, they offered the excuse that they couldn't find a fair way or honest person to distribute the food. Ephrem immediately volunteered himself. It is a sign of how respected he was that no one argued with this choice.

He and his helpers worked diligently to get food to the needy in the city and the surrounding area. It is no accident that the following verses reflect not only the physical troubles which beset Ephrem but the spiritual ones as well:

All kinds of storms trouble me—
and you have been kinder to the Ark:
only waves surrounded it,

but ramps and weapons and waves surround me....
O Helmsman of the Ark, be my pilot on dry land!
You gave the Ark rest on the haven of a mountain,
give me rest in the haven of my walls.[1]

Make a Joyful Noise
Ephrem the Deacon, known as the "Harp of the Holy Spirit," is considered by many to be one of the foremost liturgical poets that the Christian church has ever produced. In fact, some compare him to Dante, the preeminent liturgical poet of the Western Tradition. Yet Ephrem's contribution goes deeper. One of the purposes of his metrical compositions was to combat the heresies of his time. His excellent manner—at once poetic and symbolic—attracted many who had strayed from the teachings of the church back to firm Catholic belief.

For this he has been named a doctor of the church. When we think of what it takes to recognize a saint, Ephrem surely fits the bill: a man who graces worship with meaningful and orthodox song, and who tends to the needs of the poor.

St. John Chrysostom *(349–407)*
Feast day: September 13
Pope John Paul II authorized the return of the relics of St. John Chrysostom to his ancestral see of Constantinople on November 27, 2004. Looted by Crusaders in 1204 and taken to Rome, the bones of one of the most famous bishops of the universal, undivided (AD 1054) church came home to rest. This bold act furthered the possibilities for healing between the Western Church and the Eastern Churches.

Nicknamed *Chrysostomos* in Greek, meaning "The Golden-Mouthed One," John is widely recognized as one of the most eminent preachers the church has ever produced. Revered as a saint by both the Eastern and Western Churches, John was a very human

man, with struggles from within and without. Yet he attained spiritual greatness and personal sanctity worthy of imitation

Born in the fourth century in Antioch, then the third-largest city in the Roman Empire, John converted to Christianity as a young adult. He received a classical Greco-Roman education, acquiring the skills for a career in rhetoric along with a love of the Greek language and of literature.

As he grew older, he became more deeply committed to Christianity and went on to study theology under the famous teacher Diodore of Tarsus.

Love for Scripture, the Poor

John lived an extreme asceticism and became a hermit around 375. He spent the next two years continually standing—scarcely sleeping—and committed the Bible to memory. As a consequence of these practices, his stomach and kidneys were permanently damaged. Poor health forced his return to Antioch.

After recovering, John was ordained a priest (or presbyter) in 386. This event seems to have solidified the two main focuses of his life: his love of Scripture and, like St. Ephrem before him, his clear and outspoken concern for the poor. The following quote is typical of the many things John had to say:

> Do you wish to honor the body of Christ? Do not ignore him when he is naked. Do not pay him homage in the temple clad in silk, only then to neglect him outside where he is cold and ill-clad. He who said: "This is my body" is the same who said: "You saw me hungry and you gave me no food" and "Whatever you did to the least of my brothers you did also to me"....What good is it if the Eucharistic table is overloaded with golden chalices when your brother is dying of hunger? Start by satisfying his hunger and then with what is left you may adorn the altar as well.[2]

Speaking Out Against Excess

This concern for the poor deepened when, in 398, John was asked to go to Constantinople to become the chief bishop or, as properly known, patriarch. In this wealthy and decadent Roman capital, John was confronted with all that he abhorred. It wasn't long before he clashed with the Empress Eudoxia, wife of the Roman Emperor Arcadius. Used to the pleasures of the most powerful empire on earth, Eudoxia had Patriarch John banished into exile for his criticism of her lifestyle.

John died on the way to his place of exile in 407, a sad ending to his life of zeal for the gospel and concern for the poor and oppressed. Yet his martyrdom mirrored that of his master, Jesus, who died that we might live.

ST. SHARBEL MAKHLOUF *(1828–1898)*
Feast day: July 24

"Joseph, Joseph! Come out of the monastery! Come home where you belong!" cried Mrs. Makhlouf and other relatives, convinced that Joseph was making a mistake in entering the monastery. Joseph knew better.

His dedication to God and to a life of prayer was already firmly planted in his soul, and he wasn't about to leave these behind. Joseph desired to join the long procession of devout Lebanese Christians of the Maronite Catholic Church who have dedicated their lives to the service of Christ and the church through prayer and fasting within religious communities.

Joseph Makhlouf was born on May 8, 1828, in the village of Bqaaqafra in the high mountains of northern Lebanon. He was the youngest of five children born to poor, respectable and devout parents. They made sure their children were adequately fed and well educated.

Obedient and Disciplined

In 1853, after a brief time in another monastery, Joseph transferred to the Monastery of St. Maron at Annaya, where he took the name of Sharbel, an ancient martyr in the Eastern Church. It is here that the incident at the beginning of this story took place. On July 23, 1859, Brother Sharbel was ordained a priest.

Like John Chrysostom and countless others before him, Sharbel led a life of arduous asceticism. Then, in 1875, the superior of the monastery gave Fr. Sharbel permission to live as a hermit. For twenty-three more years, he did not live independently in the solitude of his hermitage but remained at the disposal of his superiors, following very strict discipline. On Christmas Eve 1898, Sharbel fell asleep in the Lord, faithful to his vision of total dedication to the Eucharist, to the Word of God in the Bible and to Mary, Mother of God.

The fame of holiness that surrounded St. Sharbel during his life spread even more after his death.

Ecumenical Spirit

Many miracles have occurred through St. Sharbel's intercession, including the fact that his body remained incorrupt for many years after his death. These were proofs that led the Vatican to declare his beatification in 1965. Pope Paul VI, who ordered the beatification to coincide with the closing of the Second Vatican Council, had in mind to propose the holy hermit Sharbel as a providential man, bearing to our modern world a message of deep spirituality of an ecumenical character.

On October 7, 1977, Pope Paul VI canonized Sharbel. His life of holiness and rigor is not for all, certainly. However, along our way to the Kingdom, such examples urge us to seriously direct our own lives to the way of the Lord.

STEPPING OUT IN FAITH

Become your best in your cultural setting. Follow in the footsteps of...

- St. Ephrem, who drew many back to the church through his music, which he used to combat heresy and clarify doctrine. Use your gifts and talents to uphold the truth. Thank someone who has inspired your growth in faith.
- St. John Chrysostom, whose love of Scripture, concern for the poor, and ascetic lifestyle led him to criticize the extravagant lifestyle of the empress. Examine your own lifestyle for excesses and make needed changes.
- St. Sharbel Makhlouf, who responded to God's call to religious life against his family's wishes and active discouragement. Encourage a member of your family or parish to consider a vocation to the priesthood or religious life. Pray for vocations.

| CHAPTER THREE |

Male Founders: Answering God's Call

Albert Haase, O.F.M.

"Come, follow me." Throughout history, every Christian has been challenged to respond to this call to follow Christ in his or her life. The response, of course, is expressed differently, depending upon the person, the historical moment and the culture involved. However, every now and then, someone comes along who gives such a unique and universal interpretation to the call of discipleship that it endures the passing of centuries and even thrives within new cultures. Each of this chapter's three male founders of religious communities offers such a lasting and adaptable response to the call of Christ.

St. Benedict of Nursia *(c. 480–547)*
Feast day: March 21

Benedict of Nursia emerged in the midst of political and church chaos and turmoil. Fifth-century Rome had fallen to the Germanic king, Alaric, and soon all of Italy was ravaged by the Goths. Heresies such as Pelagianism, the denial of the need for God's grace in overcoming sinfulness, as well as Arianism, the claim that the Son was not equal to the Father, were spreading.

Our knowledge of Benedict comes from book two of the *Dialogues* of Pope St. Gregory the Great. It's important to note that within the past three years, a respected scholar has raised serious doubt that the work was written by the hand of the sainted pope and that book two was never intended as a modern biography. Typical of medieval times, the book was designed to enlighten and inspire—not inform—with spiritual lessons taken from the life of the saint.

Tradition says that Benedict was born in the mountain village of Nursia, northeast of Rome, around 480. Sent to Rome for classical studies, he found city life not to his liking. He left Rome and settled in the mountain town of Enfide, some forty miles east.

New Directions

An encounter with Romanus, a monk from the monastery at Subiaco, gave Benedict a new direction. At the advice of the monk, Benedict became a hermit for three years. The monks of a neighboring monastery then persuaded him to become their spiritual leader. He agreed, only to quickly discover that the monks lacked enthusiasm and sincerity.

The *Dialogues* describe two murder attempts on Benedict's life, both failing as a result of his miraculous powers. Benedict left those monks and traveled south to establish twelve monasteries with twelve monks each. Around 529, he moved to Monte Cassino, destroyed a pagan temple dedicated to Apollo and built his first monastery. It was there that he wrote his famous Rule and died on March 21, 547.

Rule for Life

Benedict is not mentioned in any literature dated before the end of the sixth century. His Rule, translated more often than any other book except the Bible, has had a greater impact than Benedict himself. The Rule of St. Benedict is a masterful interpretation of how to follow Christ.

The genius of Benedict's Rule lies in its wise and compassionate blending of the rich Eastern monastic traditions with changes appropriate to contemporary times. Moderation and common sense are its hallmarks as it provides order and stability in the midst of chaotic times.

It outlines a family lifestyle within the walls of a monastery with little of the harshness and penitential practices of Eastern monasticism.

The liturgy, especially the Divine Office, plays a major daily role. Manual labor provides income and alms for the poor. Guests are welcomed as Christ. The abbot, head of the family and representative of Christ, communicates the will of God after seeking advice from his monks, especially the younger ones. Obedience, in its original meaning of listening, is the monk's primary response to the Word of God and to the abbot. One's daily life is characterized by reverence for God's continual presence and climbing the twelve rungs of humility.

Though there were many other monastic Rules in circulation at the time, the church council held at Aix-la-Chapelle in 817 proposed Benedict's as the basic Rule of western monastic life. And today, thousands of men and women, from Perth, Australia, to Pittsburgh, Pennsylvania, continue to find its meaning and message suitable for their contemporary times and culture.

ST. FRANCIS OF ASSISI *(c. 1182–1226)*
Feast day: October 4

Seven centuries later, another Italian would follow in the footprints of Christ, not behind the walls of a monastery but in the streets. Unlike the monk whose Rule left a greater impression than his personality, the charismatic person and life of Francis of Assisi would shape and outshine the Rules he left behind.

Born into the emerging merchant class of Assisi, probably in 1182, the adolescent Francis had dreams of becoming a famous knight. Those dreams were quickly dashed as he lay captured in neighboring Perugia.

Gaining his freedom and returning home to convalesce, he and the evolution of his evangelical lifestyle would be greatly influenced by significant events over the next twenty or so years. This manner of life, unique in its radical interpretation of the Gospels and obedience to the pope, consisted of voluntary poverty, care for the sick and preaching the message of Jesus to others.

The Person of Christ

Outside Assisi's walls lay a leper hospital run by the Brothers of St. Anthony. One day, on his walk outside the town, Francis encountered a leper. Surprising even himself, he embraced the leper, an event that he subsequently attributed to God's grace. Later versions of the story have the leper vanishing after the kiss.

Francis discovered in this leper the person of Christ: poor, crucified, a beggar. Following in Christ's footprints, he decided to live his life exactly in this way. And so, renouncing his family inheritance and donning the rough tunic of a penitent, he started living on the margins of society, as a beggar among his "brothers-Christ," the lepers.

People took notice and wanted to follow the same path. With about a dozen followers, Francis approached the pope for permission to preach penance and conversion. Permission was granted, and a preaching ministry developed.

According to tradition, one day some townsfolk refused to listen to Francis. So he went into the forest and preached to the birds. This incident, along with the famous song he composed toward the end of his life, "Canticle of the Creatures," gave birth to the tradition of animal stories associated with Francis. It witnesses to the brotherhood and sisterhood of all creation as a gift from the divine alms-giver.

Enduring Devotion

For Christmas 1223, in the town of Greccio, Francis combined the liturgy with an enactment of the stable scene at Bethlehem. With donkey and sheep, and with townsfolk portraying the Holy Family, Francis transformed the feast of Christmas into a celebration of the humility of God. This humility, which Francis also saw evident in the Eucharist as Jesus comes under the appearance of bread, characterizes the relationships of all Francis' followers.

In September 1224, while he made a forty-day retreat on Mount La Verna, Francis' devotion to the crucified Christ, begun in the encounter with the leper, blossomed forth in his body as God branded him with the stigmata, the very wounds of Christ. Devotion to the Crucified's love would be unique to Franciscans before entering mainstream Catholic spirituality in the sixteenth century.

So closely did Francis follow in the footprints of Christ that some fifty years after his death in 1226, he was referred to as an *alter Christus*, "another Christ." Indeed, this shows the power of his person that inspires and influences both the spirituality and religious orders that bear his name. His devotion to the crib, the Eucharist, and the cross, all suggesting God's humility and love, continues to find expression in countries and cultures from Asia to the Americas.

St. Ignatius Loyola *(1491–1556)*
Feast day: July 31

The Franciscans and Benedictines played a role in the life of the sixteenth-century founder of the Society of Jesus, the Jesuits.

Ignatius was born in the Basque province of northern Spain in 1491. As a teen, he became a page in service to the treasurer of the kingdom of Castile. In 1521, while defending the town of Pamplona against the French, he was wounded in one leg and had the other broken by a cannonball.

During his recuperation, Ignatius read the lives of the saints, including that of Francis of Assisi, and decided to imitate them. Regaining his strength but now walking with a permanent limp, he made his way to the Benedictine monastery of Montserrat. After dedicating himself to the Virgin Mary, he continued on to the Holy Land, where he hoped to convert non-Christians.

God in All Things
Ignatius' decision to spend time in a cave near the town of Manresa, Catalonia, proved crucial. The intended few days became ten months. While he was there, the ideas of what became his great gift to the history of spirituality, the *Spiritual Exercises*, took shape.

The *Exercises* are both an experience of discerning direction in life and a handbook for guiding and facilitating the experience. Designed originally as an experience for a director and an individual, the *Exercises* came to be used in groups and gave birth to the modern-day preached retreat.

Ignatius had a vision while at Manresa. Though he never described it, he said he learned more from it than he did during the rest of his life. The effect of this vision was impressive: Ignatius was able to find God in all things. All of Jesuit spirituality flows from this grace.

Arriving in the Turkish-held Holy Land where the situation was tense and dangerous, he was ordered to leave by the Franciscan who had authority over Catholics. Returning to Spain, Ignatius began studies in Latin with the hope of becoming a priest. After classes, he began explaining the Gospels and teaching prayer to fellow students and others. He attracted the attention of the Spanish Inquisition for suspected heresy and was thrown into jail. He moved to another city and was jailed again, this time by the Dominicans; he left Spain for Paris to continue his studies for the priesthood.

Serving the Pope

His roommates at the University of Paris were Francis Xavier and Peter Faber. Along with four other students, they took vows of poverty and chastity. Thinking of themselves more as individual priests than as a religious order, they placed themselves at the service of the pope in 1538. The pope commissioned them to teach theology and Scripture and to preach.

Ignatius' companions met in Rome the following Lent. After weeks of prayer and discussion, they formed a community in service to the pope. This became a vow in addition to the traditional vows of poverty, chastity, and obedience. A reluctant Ignatius was unanimously elected superior general of the new Society of Jesus in 1541. Ignatius spent the next fifteen years, until his death in 1556, composing the Constitutions of the Society as well as writing letters to Jesuits as close as Italy and Portugal and as far away as Brazil and Japan.

Though Ignatius had no intention of including education as a ministry of the Society, requests by rulers and bishops soon gave birth to what the Jesuits are best known for today.

They teach to fulfill their motto, *Ad Majorem Dei Gloriam,* ("to the greater glory of God").

STEPPING OUT IN FAITH

Respond to Christ's call in a lasting and intentional way. Follow in the footsteps of...

- St. Benedict of Nursia, who wrote a Rule of Life that has guided many in their following of Christ. Write down your own "Rule" for your life. Share it with your family, friends, or small faith community.
- St. Francis of Assisi, who discovered the person of Christ in a leper and the humility of Christ in his birth in a stable. Explore the "lowly" persons and places where Christ may be found in your life. Evaluate who you try to impress, and why.
- St. Ignatius Loyola, whose Spiritual Exercises led to modern-day preached retreats. Plan to participate in a retreat or make a commitment of time to spiritual reading and prayer to discern the direction of the next phase of your life.

| CHAPTER FOUR |

Female Founders: Answering God's Call

Vicky Hébert and Denis Sabourin

Three holy women, Sts. Clare of Assisi, Julie Billiart, and Angela Merici, each one was ahead of her time. Dedicated to serving the Lord, they recognized societal needs and sought remedies for these concerns. Each founded a religious order of women with the intent of bringing education to women and care to society's poor and marginalized. Their timeless message of compassion for the needy reaches out and grabs us by the heart. It is as pertinent and timely today as it was in their days.

St. Clare of Assisi *(c. 1194–1253)*

Feast day: August 11

Chiara Favarone was born around 1194, in Assisi, Italy, the eldest daughter of a noble family. Her devout mother, Ortolana, named her Chiara (meaning "light") following a revelatory dream in which Ortolana was told she would give birth to the "light which would illuminate the world."

The teenaged Chiara, or Clare, heard Francis of Assisi passionately preach about new ways of living the gospel. His words reached right to Clare's soul: She vowed to answer the Lord's call. Francis became her confidant and spiritual guide.

As was tradition, Clare's uncle tried to arrange an advantageous marriage for her. Refusing all suitors, Clare ran away and sought refuge with Francis and his community. He immediately accepted her into the gospel life. She received a tonsure, promised obedience to Francis, and lived very briefly with neighboring Benedictine sisters who gave her sanctuary.

Her sister Agnes soon joined Clare, who was then living in another religious house nearby. They soon moved to San Damiano, the small chapel outside of Assisi in which Francis had heard the Lord's call. Clare worked with Agnes (now St. Agnes of Assisi) and others who joined them to found the Order of Poor Ladies (Poor Clares). They provided a place for women who felt called to live a humble life of prayer and hard work and to share what they had with those in need.

An Intentional Life
Adopting austere practices, eating little meat, speaking only when necessary and living in strict poverty, the members of the new foundation eventually become enclosed. Clare's Order depended on alms for both subsistence and the ability to travel to establish new foundations. Their lack of land-based revenue was a new concept.

Clare was appointed abbess in 1216. Following Agnes's example, Clare's mother, Blessed Ortolana, her younger sister, Beatrice, and other relatives joined the group at San Damiano. Clare considered Francis her spiritual father; she was his confidante and cared for him during his last illness before his death in 1226.

In 1234, the convent at San Damiano faced attack by marauding soldiers. Rising from her sickbed, Clare carried the Blessed Sacrament to where the soldiers would see it. Asking the Lord to hear her prayers and save her sisters, she heard the following reply: "I will protect them as I always have and always will." History recounts that the soldiers retreated from the area, never attacking San Damiano.

Shining Example

Clare died on August 11, 1253, just two days after Pope Innocent IV confirmed Clare's Rule. She was fifty-nine. She was canonized two years later in 1255. The Poor Ladies' name was officially changed to the Order of Saint Clare in 1263. Today they are commonly known as Poor Clares.

In 1958, Pope Pius XII designated Clare as the patron saint of television as a result of an event near the end of her life. Clare was bedridden and too ill to attend Mass, but she was able to see—miraculously—the Mass on the wall of her room! The scope of Clare's patronage also includes communication services (telephone, telegraph, and TV writers), eyes, eye diseases, needle workers, goldsmiths, launderers, and good weather.

Today, the Poor Clares number approximately seventeen thousand sisters living in about a thousand monasteries/convents in sixty-seven countries. Their timeless dedication to contemplative prayer for others and refusal to rely upon worldly goods provide a shining example of piety, love of the Lord, and faith in the twenty-first century and beyond.[1]

St. Julie Billiart *(1751–1816)*

Feast day: April 8

It was the poor and abandoned who touched the heart of Julie Billiart. It was they who prompted her to found the Congregation of the Sisters of Notre Dame de Namur, devoted to the Christian education of girls, the training of teachers and to making God's goodness known.

Marie-Rose-Julie, the seventh of eight children, was born July 12, 1751, in Cuvilly, France, to a farmer and his wife. Julie loved attending her one-room school. She excelled in the religious instruction offered by the parish priest. He recognized her remarkable devotion and allowed her to make her First Communion at the early age of nine.

A constant help to her parents, in her spare time Julie gathered the local children to teach them the catechism and read gospel stories to them. At the age of fourteen, she took a private vow of chastity, dedicating her life to serve the Lord by teaching the poor.

Troubled Times

In 1774, when Julie was twenty-three years old, she was seated next to her father when a gunshot rang out. The shot had been fired into their home! Was it an accident or an attempted murder of her father? The shock of the event left Julie paralyzed, a painful condition she would have for most of her adult life.

Julie, ever devout, spent long hours in prayer. People from all walks of life came to seek her counsel in her humble home. She soon came to be known as "la devoté" for encouraging the people to refuse to accept the schismatic priest in the parish.

The terrors of the French Revolution forced Julie to relocate to Amiens, where she met Françoise Blin de Bourdon, the Viscountess of Gazaincourt, who had suffered during the Reign of Terror (September 1793 to July 1794). The two devoted women became inseparable friends and coworkers in their desire to restore religion and the faith of the people through education.

In 1803, at the request of the bishop of Amiens, Julie and Françoise welcomed eight orphans to their first classes in their small convent. On February 2, 1804, Julie, Françoise, and another woman consecrated themselves as a community to serve the poor and the abandoned. Fr. Varin, their spiritual adviser, gave them a provisional rule which, it is said, was so ahead of its time that its essential aspects have never needed to be changed. In June 1804, Julie was cured of her paralysis while she made a novena in obedience to her confessor. Sixteen months later, Julie and Françoise, along with a handful of other interested young women, took their first vows as a community.

How Good God Is!

The founding of the Sisters of Notre Dame did not proceed without its disagreements with various church leaders, one of which resulted in the relocation of their motherhouse to Namur, Belgium, in 1809.

Mother Julie spent her declining years caring for soldiers injured at the Battle of Waterloo (1815). In January of 1816, Mother Julie fell gravely ill. After three months of pain, she died praying the Magnificat. She was sixty-five.

Mother Julie Billiart was beatified in 1906 and canonized in 1969. This woman of vision—often heard uttering, *"Ah, qu'il est bon, le bon Dieu!"* ("Oh, how good the good God is!")—is the patroness of catechists. St. Julie's vision is alive in the approximately two thousand Sisters of Notre Dame who serve on five continents.[2]

St. Angela Merici *(1474–1540)*

Finding God in daily life, serving God in people around her, Angela Merici created a surprising new way of life. Her spiritual family now includes the Company of St. Ursula for single women and the Order of St. Ursula for women religious.

Angela grew up on her family's farm in northern Italy, where she was born around 1474. She and her siblings worked together and got in trouble together. Listening as their father read the lives of the saints, Angela longed to imitate these friends of God.

Death ruptured this happy circle, first taking her older sister. Angela was devastated—and worried. Was her mischievous sister in heaven? One day, she had a consoling experience: Angela saw her sister, happy in heaven.

Still a teenager, Angela lost both parents. While her older brothers tried to keep up the farm, she and a younger brother went to live with an uncle and aunt who were eager to arrange a marriage for her. Their plans and Angela's vocation were on a collision course.

Angela sensed God's call to a deep intimacy with him. The more her guardians tried to find a husband, the more she resisted.

She sought guidance from Franciscan friars and joined the Third Order (now called the Secular Franciscan Order) for laypersons. Its spiritual practices deepened her prayer life. Finally, her family accepted Angela's desire to devote herself to God alone.

Woman of Compassion and Wisdom

Soon she was back on the farm. One day during the olive harvest, Angela had another visionary experience: women and angels on a ladder between heaven and earth. She understood that someday she would establish a group of women consecrated to God.

Meanwhile, Angela's days began with Mass and were punctuated by prayer. She worked with neighbors and helped out where needed. People turned to her for wisdom and comfort. The sadness of her own losses had taught her deep compassion for others. When the friars asked her to console a widow whose three children had died, Angela visited her in the war-torn city of Brescia. This became the place for her life's work.

Soon Brescians discovered Angela's goodness and wisdom. Husband and wife quarrelling? Talk with Angela! Should I propose marriage? Consult Angela! Doubts about faith? Turn to Angela! One time she persuaded two sworn enemies to call off a duel.

A New Path for Women

Angela encouraged women and men who were caring for orphans and the dying, trying to heal their ravaged city. She encountered other single women who knew that God was calling them, but not to marriage or religious life—the only paths open to women at that time. They wanted to learn from her experience of intimacy with God. On November 25, 1535, Angela and twenty-eight other women consecrated themselves to Christ under the patronage of St. Ursula, an early martyr and leader of women.

By her death in 1540, the Company of St. Ursula had a hundred and fifty members.

Ursulines still live as Angela did, dedicated to Christ and serving others in ordinary circumstances, as single laywomen. The Company of St. Ursula now exists in twenty countries.

The Company spread throughout Italy and into France. There, in the early 1600s, French Ursulines took another step, becoming a religious order. These women pioneered education for young women; their life and mission has spread around the globe. St. Angela Merici was canonized in 1807.[3]

STEPPING OUT IN FAITH

Dedicate your life to serving the Lord. Follow in the footsteps of…

- St. Clare of Assisi, who depended on the generosity of others for the support of her community. Learn more about the Poor Clare community in your area, join them for liturgy and support them with your own generosity.
- St. Julie Billiart, who worked to make God's goodness known during a time of war and social upheaval. Make her prayer "Oh, how good the good God is!" your own and see how it helps you to be an agent of peace in our world.
- St. Angela Merici, whose early experiences of loss helped her to have compassion for others. Reach out in support of another who is experiencing a difficulty you have encountered in your life.

CHAPTER FIVE

Companions in Faith

Mitch and Kathy Finley

Read your way through just about any volume of lives of the saints and you may conclude that you're unlikely to become a saint if you develop a long-term friendship with a member of the opposite sex. You could think this, however, only if you overlook that more than a few saints are examples of just the opposite. Indeed, these saints' friendships—that they shared themselves with each other on a more-than-superficial level—contributed in significant ways to the fact that the grace of God accomplished surpassing holiness in their lives.

St. Francis de Sales *(1567–1622)*
Feast day: January 29

St. Jane Frances de Chantal *(1572–1641)*
Feast day: August 12
From a distinguished family, Jane de Chantal was the daughter of a prominent lawyer, the president of the parliament of the Burgundy region of France. Her husband, with whom she had a happy marriage, was the baron of Chantal. Her brother was the archbishop of Bourges. Jane gave birth to six children, but only a boy and two girls lived past early infancy.

In 1601, Jane's husband was killed in a hunting accident, and for three years thereafter she was deeply depressed. A priest offered to become Jane's spiritual director, and she accepted gratefully. But as things developed, this priest was no great blessing. Jane struggled under his harsh and insensitive influence.

Jane de Chantal met Francis de Sales for the first time in 1604, when Francis was the thirty-seven-year-old bishop of Geneva, Switzerland, and Jane was a thirty-two-year-old noblewoman and widow with three children, living with her father in Dijon, France. During Lent that year, Francis gave a series of public sermons in Dijon which Jane attended and which affected her deeply.

Francis' kindness and wisdom touched Jane's heart. Aware that she needed spiritual help, Jane was able to meet with Francis and tell him of her situation. Francis sympathized, but he felt that he could not lightly take over Jane's spiritual direction from another priest. After much prayer, however, Francis informed Jane that the other priest had accomplished nothing but to destroy her conscience. Thereupon, Jane made her confession to Francis, which resulted in a feeling of deep joy and freedom of heart.

As a spiritual director, Francis de Sales respected the life experience of those he directed. He was a good listener, and he refused to set himself up in the place of God "for fear," he said, "of harming souls."

In the beginning, Jane was mystified because Francis did not give her a set of firm rules to follow. Soon, however, she began to appreciate Francis' gentle style. "Never," she later recalled, "did that blessed one make quick replies." Rather, he knew that God's love was at work in Jane and that both he and she must be patient.

After Francis' return to Geneva, the two corresponded regularly. In one letter, Francis advised, "As regards devotions, I should approve of your still going slow." It was three years before the two met again, near Pentecost 1607. Jane put her life in Francis' hands, but he advised waiting patiently while she found her own answers.[1]

Jane felt called to join an order of women religious, but at the time religious orders demanded a life of such austerity that Francis advised against them all. There was a need, Francis said, for a new kind of religious community for women, "not too mild for the strong, nor too harsh for the weak." It would be a community for women unable to join any of the existing orders because of their age, poor health, or need to care for children, and it would be especially appropriate for widows. These women religious would maintain their ties of affection with their families.

Later, Francis wrote his spiritual classic, *On the Love of God*, for the community that Jane established near Anneçy. Wanting to emphasize the contemplative prayer that would be at the heart of community life—rather than the life of active service that Francis had proposed—Jane named her community the Daughters of the Visitation of St. Mary, or Visitandines—a reference to the visit of Mary to her cousin Elizabeth and Mary's praying of the Magnificat (see Luke 1:39–56).

It was a great blow to Jane when Francis died in 1622, but with time and prayer she regained her spiritual equilibrium and carried on. Later in life, Jane suffered great spiritual aridity and anguish, but she remained firm in her faith. By 1635 there were sixty-five Visitandine convents, and Jane worked tirelessly to nurture them all.

It was on her way back to Anneçy from a visit to one of the convents that Jane became ill and died on December 13, 1641. Her body was taken to Anneçy where she was buried near her beloved friend, Francis.

St. Vincent de Paul *(c. 1580 –1660)*
Feast day: September 27

St. Louise de Marillac *(1591–1660)*
Feast day: March 15

Vincent de Paul is familiar to us because of the thousands of social service agencies, in more than a hundred and thirty countries, that bear his name. Many don't realize, however, that Louise de Marillac worked closely with Vincent in serving the poor in seventeenth-century France. Vincent was born about 1580 to a peasant family. Louise was born out of wedlock on August 12, 1591.

Vincent de Paul and Louise de Marillac met in 1623, and he agreed to be her spiritual director, even though his overriding concern was to serve the poor. Initially, she thought Vincent was rigid and distant. Gradually, however, the two became close friends.

When Louise's dull, anger-prone husband died on December 21, 1625, she decided that she would not marry again. Louise lived in a little apartment and spent much time in prayer. She painted watercolors, knitted for Vincent's poor people, and sewed vestments for Vincent. Vincent pleaded with Louise not to work so hard and not to burden herself with pious devotions and disciplines.

In her late thirties by this time, Louise had never known any human warmth, but she knew that she had to figure out what to do with herself. Gifted with practical wisdom when it came to spiritual issues, Vincent told Louise that he would not tell her what to do; she would have to figure it out for herself. Finally, more than two years later, Louise began to get her act together.

Vincent had established groups of upper-class women, which he called the Ladies of Charity, who cared for the poor and the sick. In 1628, Vincent asked Louise to travel about to inspect his growing charity activities, and Louise realized that she possessed talents she had never known she had.

She wrote out detailed reports for Vincent and, before long, she became a management whiz.

In each place she found someone to teach the children to read because she believed that literacy was the key to improving people's lives. She also became a captivating public speaker.

In a few places Louise met opposition, even from the local clergy who accused her of trying to do their work, but, for the most part, the people welcomed and supported her.

Most of the Ladies of Charity were reluctant to serve the poor directly. They would send money or a servant instead. So Louise decided to recruit hearty country girls, who had common sense and didn't shy away from work. She would train them in religion and nursing. On November 26, 1633, she welcomed her first four recruits.

At every opportunity, Vincent supported Louise and offered advice. When Louise's difficult son needed help to become self-sufficient, Vincent found him work. Later, he solicited enough money from Louise's father's family for the young man to marry. About this time, Louise named her fledgling community the Daughters of Charity. She drew up statutes, and Vincent gave them his approval. The women of the community learned prayer, meditation, basic nursing skills, and practical ways to help the poor. They wore peasant clothes rather than a traditional religious habit.

Because most of the Daughters of Charity were not well educated, Vincent and Louise held conferences once or twice a month, and all the Daughters were encouraged to join the conversation. Over time, Vincent stepped away from the work of the Daughters of Charity, confident that Louise could take care of it. The two had a long and affectionate friendship, and they continued to correspond until Louise died on March 16, 1660.

Vincent followed her in death on September 27 of the same year.

STEPPING OUT IN FAITH

Share your life with faithful friends. Follow in the footsteps of...

- St. Francis de Sales, whose gentleness and listening ear invited Jane Frances de Chantal's trust. Patiently listen to a friend in need.
- St. Jane Frances de Chantal, who sought her friend Francis de Sales's guidance yet trusted herself about the kind of religious community to form. Seek advice from others, but also trust God's guidance and your own heart.
- St. Vincent de Paul, who refrained from solving Louise de Marillac's problems and challenged her to sort things out herself. Give your friends the space they need to grow in confidence in their own abilities.
- St. Louise de Marillac, who moved beyond her negative impression of Vincent de Paul to become his friend. Have you made unfair or hasty judgments of others? Could you be missing out on a good friendship?

CHAPTER SIX

Men and Women Who Changed the Church
William H. Shannon

In his classic work, *Seeds of Contemplation*, Thomas Merton wonders if there are twenty living persons who see things as they are, who are free from material attachments and who are ever responsive to God's grace and aware of God's presence. There must be a few, he believes: "They are the ones who are holding everything together and keeping the universe from falling apart."

An exaggerated portrait of a saint by an enthusiastic young monk? Perhaps. Yet there is truth in what he says. A person who comes even close to Merton's description would surely be an influence for good on a small—and sometimes large—scale, changing the world. We feature here several people who left a large legacy.

St. Ambrose *(339–397)*
Feast day: December 7
Suppose you picked up your morning paper and read the front-page headline: "Governor Chosen as Catholic Bishop." It is an understatement to say that you would be astounded, perhaps wondering whether it might be an early April Fool's Day joke. In truth, it is something that actually happened centuries ago in Milan, Italy.

In 374, the bishop of the city died, and people gathered to choose his successor. (In those days, bishops were chosen by the local laity and clergy.) It was a disquieting time in Milan. The church was bitterly divided between Nicene Christians (who believed in the divinity of Christ) and the Arians (who taught that Jesus was only human). Hot tempers raised the specter of violence and bloodshed.

Ambrose—who in 370 had left the practice of law to become the governor of the Western Empire—arrived on the scene and addressed the crowd, calling for order and peace. Suddenly, as if from nowhere, a voice was heard, chanting: "Ambrose for bishop!" This chant was taken up by the people. Ambrose was horrified.

At the time he was a catechumen, not yet baptized. Still, the people insisted, and in short order he was baptized, ordained, and made bishop of Milan.

Rising to the Task

There were not then (and, it would seem, still are not) wise courses on how to be a bishop. But Ambrose was a quick learner. He listened to credible teachers and steeped himself in the Scriptures and in the writings of early Christian teachers, such as Origen, Basil, Athanasius, and others. Even though Ambrose is now a doctor of the church, he is less remembered for his writings than for the striking model he offered of a truly pastoral bishop ministering generously to all, and especially to the poor.

His was no easy task; his career as bishop was a stormy one. He had troubles with the Arians, whose request for a church building in Milan he had to refuse. He had trouble with the Roman Emperor Theodosius, who, in reprisal for the death of the governor of Thessalonica, had ordered the merciless massacre of thousands of men, women and children in that city. Ambrose ordered the emperor to do public penance—and the emperor obeyed. Ambrose told Theodosius: "The emperor is in the Church, not above it."

A Legacy of Peace and Wisdom

In 476, less than a century after Ambrose's death, the Roman Empire fell into the hands of invaders from the north. In his day, Ambrose had already seen signs of decline, as violence and lawlessness crept through the empire. The only defense against the increasing chaos was the army, for there were no police or courts of law to defend human rights and work for peace.

In this critical context, it is quite understandable that Ambrose became one of the architects of the just war theory that was destined to become the classic Catholic attitude toward war for centuries. Only in our day—times very different from Ambrose's—has this approach to war been widely questioned.

His wisdom and deep learning helped prepare St. Augustine—that intellectual giant of the Western Church—to accept Christian faith. This may well be Ambrose's most enduring gift to the church.

St. Athanasius *(296–373)*

Feast day: May 2

The other day, a second-grade teacher showed me a list of questions her pupils had asked about God. Among the questions were these: "How old is God?" and "Is there a Spanish God?" One child's question especially caught my attention. She asked: "Was Jesus God?" This question really struck me, probably because I had been thinking of writing this article on St. Athanasius. It was this same question that haunted Athanasius much of his life. It was his strong and resolute yes to it that defines much of his life story.

As a young priest in Alexandria, Egypt, Athanasius accompanied his bishop, Alexander, to the Council of Nicaea. A meeting of bishops had been called to consider the teaching of Arius, who was also a priest of the church of Alexandria. Arius taught that Jesus was not divine by nature. Though he is called Son of God in Scripture, Arians held that Jesus did not always exist and was therefore a creature, though the first of all creatures.

A Divisive Issue

After much debate, Arianism was condemned by the bishops at this first ecumenical council, which met in AD 325 in Nicaea (now Iznik in modern Turkey). Though it was condemned, Arianism did not disappear: It continued to be a divisive issue in the church for more than half a century. Arius was a brilliant propagandist who succeeded in creating a large following throughout the Christian church, especially at the imperial court.

Three years after the Council, Athanasius was elected as the bishop of Alexandria. In his capacity as bishop, he strongly defended the decision of Nicaea and refused to compromise with the Arians. His tenure as bishop was a long one: forty-three years. For seventeen of those years he was away from the seat of his diocese, not by choice but because, on five different occasions, he was forced into exile. Several times this was at the order of the Emperor Constantius, whom Arius had won over to his cause. Athanasius was exiled to Trier, to Rome, and into the Egyptian desert several times.

An Extraordinary Man

Cardinal John Henry Newman, who wrote an extensive history of the church in the nineteen century, saw Athanasius as a shining light in that troubled period when Arianism almost succeeded in replacing the orthodox teaching of Nicaea in the fourth century. St. Jerome described that period when he wrote (with some exaggeration perhaps): "The world woke up one day and found itself Arian." Newman described Athanasius as an extraordinary man who was the instrument after the apostles by which the truths of Christianity became secure for the world.

Apart from his relentless defense of Nicaea against the Arians, Athanasius was also instrumental in making known to the rest of the church the story of those persons who, beginning in the third century, retreated from the world to live as hermits in the Egyptian desert. During his time of exile there, he came to know these desert fathers, of whom St. Anthony is a notable representative. He set himself to write their story, which he did in the *Life of St. Anthony*, a work well known and much read in the Middle Ages. It was this work that influenced the development of the monastic life in the Western Church.

St. Teresa of Avila *(1515–1582)*
Feast day: October 15

In 1492, Christopher Columbus sailed westward from Spain hoping to discover a new route to the East. He ended up discovering a new world that, until then, Europeans did not know existed. Twenty-three years later, in the fortified Spanish city of Avila, a child was born who, through her life and writings, would help people discover a new inner world that can be found only by prayer and contemplation.

Born into an aristocratic family, Teresa showed signs of a precocious spiritual piety as a child, even playing at being a hermit on the family property. At the age of seven, she tried to persuade her brother, Rodrigo, to join her in journeying to northern Africa so they could become martyrs.

Her plan was thwarted by her uncle, who met them as they were leaving the family home and summarily forced them to return.

It was not long, however, before Teresa's childish piety was displaced by a teenager's vanity. She was attractive and she knew it. She delighted in nice clothes and fine perfumes, in flirting with boys, in dancing. Her reading turned to books of chivalry and romance. But after a serious illness that grounded her for about a year and a half, she chose to become a nun and entered the Carmelite Convent of the Incarnation in Avila. She was twenty years of age.

At the time, the Convent of the Incarnation had something of a country-club aura: The nuns had frequent visitors and felt free to leave the enclosure whenever they wished. Despite the laxity that prevailed, Teresa made some effort at a life of prayer.

A Desire for More

In 1562, at the age of forty-seven and dissatisfied with the mediocrity of the religious life she had been living, she made plans to found a convent that would adhere strictly to the original form of the Carmelite Rule. The first convent she founded was St. Joseph's of Avila in 1562. From then on, Teresa's life was an amazing combination of deep prayer and remarkable efficiency as she went about founding seventeen additional convents of the reformed, or discalced (barefooted), Carmelites.

Teresa was a woman of ready wit and cheery disposition. We know about her thinking and her activities through her writings. Under obedience to her confessor, she wrote the story of her life. She also composed the *Book of Foundations,* a quite readable account of the establishment of her convents, and *The Way of Perfection,* which offered spiritual counsel for her sisters.

Moving Toward the Center

Her most mature work on the life of prayer and contemplation is *The Interior Castle.* For Teresa, the interior castle is the very center within a person where God dwells. The spiritual journey is an effort to reach that center, to achieve the deepest possible awareness of that divine presence. This takes place gradually as a person moves through the different mansions (or rooms) of the castle to that center, where one attains union with God.

As we move toward the center, prayer becomes more and more God's action in us rather than something we simply do. God brings us into wondrous union with the divine Self. We experience God's love and come to realize that the important thing in prayer is not to think much but to love much. Love brings joy. That is why Teresa could say: "God protect me from gloomy saints." In 1970, St. Teresa of Avila was declared a doctor of the church.

> ### STEPPING OUT IN FAITH
> Be an influence for good in your corner of the world! Follow in the footsteps of...
>
> - St. Ambrose, who rose to the task of a new responsibility and was generous to the poor. Reach out to an agency that serves the poor and volunteer your assistance. Don't wait to be asked. Step up!
> - St. Athanasius, who took a countercultural stand against a false teaching. Have you been silent about something that you know is wrong? Take a stand for what's right even if others oppose you.
> - St. Teresa of Avila, a person of joy, who invited others to a richer relationship with God through prayer. Has your prayer been haphazard and unscheduled? Commit to pray ten minutes a day and discover the joy it brings.

CHAPTER SEVEN

Special Friends of the Poor

Mary Cummins Wlodarski

The twenty-fifth chapter of Matthew's Gospel tells us how to reach heaven. The sheep and goats are separated, waiting to see who gets in. The requirements are simple: Did we feed the hungry, clothe the naked, visit the imprisoned? Our ticket in: Whenever we do any of these, we do them for the Lord.

Befriending the poor isn't an optional activity for Christians; it's the main event! Sts. Elizabeth of Hungary, Frances of Rome, and Martin of Tours each rejected a life of affluence and saw Jesus in those around them. Each of us must also ask, "Lord, when did I see you hungry?"

ST. ELIZABETH OF HUNGARY *(1207–1231)*
Feast day: November 17
The title of princess is mythical. A princess lives in a castle, wears beautiful clothes, and marries a handsome prince. St. Elizabeth of Hungary was born into this life in 1207.

The daughter of King Alexander II and Queen Gertrude, Elizabeth spent her earliest years surrounded by luxury. At the age of four she was betrothed to a boy of equal wealth. But Elizabeth, from an age too young to know such seriousness, was a solemn child. She was quiet and prayerful, qualities no doubt influenced by

47

the murder of her mother when she was six years old. Her faith offered her solace and healing. At fourteen, Elizabeth married Louis of Thuringia. They were well-suited and grew to love and admire one another.

Elizabeth's spirituality and pious practices, already well developed, continued. She refused to wear her jeweled crown since Jesus wore only a crown of thorns. When all others had to bow before her, she would prostrate herself in front of the chapel crucifix. In place of rich foods and wine, she fasted; instead of silk and lace, she wore the rough-woven fabrics of peasants. It's not hard to imagine the castle residents shaking their heads in amazement or clicking their tongues in derision!

Compassionate to the Core
Most confusing for many people was her attitude toward the poor and infirm. The compassionate queen ordered that a hospital be built to serve the ill and dying. Others in power sent out alms only through servants for fear of contagion or attack. In a gesture both fearless and kind, Elizabeth went into the villages and homes of her people.

A popular story of the queen's life reveals that even her loving husband did not always understand her. Concerned, King Louis asked her to cease her deliveries outside the castle walls. Elizabeth, unable to comply but unwilling to worry him, decided to sneak bread out, hiding the loaves in the folds of her dress.

Louis caught her in the act and asked to see what she had hidden. Elizabeth loosened the folds, and roses—not bread—tumbled onto the ground. Recognizing a miracle, Louis never again tried to stop his wife and joined her in her missions.

Service and Prayer
Louis and Elizabeth had two children, Hermann and Sophia, and were expecting their third when Louis went off to the Crusades. Shortly after their daughter Gertrude's birth, Elizabeth received

word of Louis's death. Now a twenty-year-old widow, she grieved sorely. The year was 1227. Francis of Assisi, who had died just the year before, would lead Elizabeth to her next stage of life.

Followers of Francis made their settlement in Germany in 1221, and had moved into Hungary with Elizabeth's help. Elizabeth was impressed with their lives of chastity, humility, and charity, so she resisted pressure to remarry and instead joined the Third Order of St. Francis. She renounced all titles and authority (which pleased those in power since they wanted to be rid of her) and served the rest of her short life in charitable efforts and prayer.

Elizabeth of Hungary died in 1231. She was only twenty-four years old. Yet, at her canonization several years later, Pope Gregory IX called her one of the greatest women of his time. She is usually shown wearing a crown and holding roses or giving alms, and she is the patron of beggars and charitable societies.

St. Frances of Rome *(1384–1440)*
Feast day: March 9

Frances was born in Rome in 1384, the only child of a noble family. She modeled her mother's deep, quiet faith, and was certain at age eleven that she wanted to enter religious life. But Frances' parents, Paul and Jacobella, had already promised her to a young aristocrat. At twelve years of age, Frances reluctantly became the wife of Lorenzo.

The shy, pensive Frances was thrust into social obligations requiring her to attend and host functions. Her health gave way, and she was bedridden for months. In an early vision, one of many she would experience, she was asked whether she wished life or death, and she graciously replied, "God's will is mine." She resolved to commit her life to spiritual growth and charitable acts. Once recovered, however, Frances was expected to resume her life as a prosperous young matron, a role she did not enjoy.

God's Generosity

Fortunately, Frances became friends with her brother-in-law's wife, Vannozza, who also wanted more than a pampered existence. They attended Mass together, visited prisons and served in hospitals. They were subjected to ridicule among their social rank, causing their mutual mother-in-law to implore her sons to control their wives.

Frances' generosity demonstrated God's generosity. Frances and Vannozza gave away so much food during a famine in Rome that their father-in-law was angry about the depleted family supplies. He hid all extra food and wine, leaving just enough for their immediate needs.

The two women went out to beg for food for the poor. When they did not collect enough, Frances scoured the family corn loft for what little she could find. Lorenzo, following her, was amazed to find the previously vacant space now filled with fresh yellow corn! Then, when Frances's miserly father-in-law complained to her about the empty wine barrel, Frances opened the tap and wine flowed in abundance. After such bounty and grace, Lorenzo and his father were converted.

Practical Compassion

Frances faced great personal sorrow, too. Rome was torn by violence and devastated by the plague. Of her three children, one was taken hostage with his father in battle, and two died of the plague. Frances, consoled by her visions of angels, became more dedicated to the poor and sick. When Lorenzo returned home, broken in body and spirit, she nursed him with other victims of the fighting.

Her example inspired many women of Rome, and others came to help. Frances started a lay order of women called the Oblates of Mary. These women continued to live in the world but dedicated themselves to serving God by serving the poor. They purchased a house so that the widows among them might have a home.

After forty years of marriage, Lorenzo died. Frances moved in with the Oblates and became their superior. It is said that angels traveled with her in the evening, lighting her way and keeping her safe on her merciful journeys. For this reason, she is considered the patron saint of automobiles, though she lived long before their invention.

Frances died in Rome in 1440, surrounded by Oblates. St. Frances of Rome is represented with an angel and a basket of food. Her mystical spirituality and practical compassion make her an example for us today, who are still plagued by violence and war.

ST. MARTIN OF TOURS *(c. 316–397)*
Feast day: November 11

Our final friend of the poor, St. Martin of Tours, was born when the church was still in its infancy. We know much of his life because a devoted follower, Sulpicius Severus, became his biographer and actually interviewed Martin and many who knew him.

Martin was born to a Roman army officer and his wife, both pagans. The persecutions of Christians had ended, but many still mistrusted this new belief in Jesus. Martin, however, at only ten, went secretly to the Christians to be admitted to the catechumenate.

He was still an unbaptized catechumen when he was forced into the Roman army at fifteen. Though he became an officer like his father before him, Martin was not seduced by status. Instead, he tried to live a simple, humble life. His call was to act as Jesus had acted.

Soldier of Christ

Martin's compassion for the poor and needy was wholehearted. As he entered the gates of the garrison one particularly cold winter day, he spied a freezing beggar, nearly naked in the cruel wind. In one quick stroke, Martin took his sword and sliced his own cape in half, handing one piece to the man and keeping the other for himself. He was ridiculed within the ranks for his clownish appearance, but that night Martin dreamed Jesus came to him, wearing half of the cape!

Martin, then eighteen, immediately went forward with his baptism. He decided not to draw his sword again but to become a soldier of Christ.

When it came time to name a new bishop of Tours, the people (who at that time chose their own bishops) knew they already had a holy leader in Martin. They also knew that Martin, in his humility, would never willingly accept the position.

The townspeople tricked him into visiting a sick woman and dragged him to be consecrated. He gave in but never lived in a palace as other bishops did. At first he lived in a monk's small cell and later in a hermitage outside the city. His identification with the poor and powerless was rooted in his desire to follow the example of Jesus.

Martin was committed to reaching out to those who did not believe in Christ. This man, who really desired only contemplation and solitude, gave up both. He traveled from village to village and even preached door-to-door.

Commitment to Care
Showing his great courage and persistence, Martin often intervened when political leaders were oppressive or violent. Once, he learned that a general named Avitianus had come to Tours with prisoners whom he planned to torture and execute. Martin arrived at Avitianus's doorstep and, though it was after midnight, stayed camped on the threshold. An angel awakened Avitianus from his sleep and told him Martin was outside. His servants persuaded the general that he was dreaming, but after he fell back asleep, the angel roused him a second time. Avitianus then went out to meet

Martin, saying, "Don't even say a word. I know what your request is. Every prisoner will be spared."

Martin died in Tours. He is considered the patron of soldiers, the poor, and the imprisoned. St. Martin's compassion for the needy, his advocacy for the weak and forgotten, and his tireless devotion to serving his people made him one of the church's most famous early saints.

STEPPING OUT IN FAITH

Befriend the poor and reject affluent living. Follow in the footsteps of...

- St. Elizabeth of Hungary, who went among the poor offering assistance. Do more than write a check or donate food and clothing. Deliver your donations and offer to help an organization that serves the needy.
- St. Frances of Rome, who shared her passion for serving the poor, first with Vannozza, her sister-in-law, and later with the Oblates of Mary. Find a friend, family member or group to support and challenge you in serving God by serving the poor.
- St. Martin of Tours, who encountered detours and surprises, yet who persisted in his calling. Name the obstacles that block your way to living as God is calling you—especially in response to the needy. Identify one obstacle you can change from a stumbling block into a stepping-stone.

CHAPTER EIGHT

Contemplatives and Mystics

Albert Haase, O.F.M.

The cross stands center stage in Christian spirituality. It symbolizes the uncompromising death to self and the courageous surrender to God that were hallmarks of Jesus' life. Every disciple must pick up his or her cross and follow in the Master's footsteps. Indeed, embracing the cross is the distinguishing act which separates Christians from other believers. All the saints have trod the *via dolorosa,* the way of sorrows.

This chapter's trio of saints each experienced the cross in such a profound way that they are called "mystics"—people who had a unique experience of and response to God in the depths of their suffering.

St. Thérèse of Lisieux *(1873–1897)*

Feast day: October 1

She was dead at the age of twenty-four. She spent the last decade of her life behind the walls of a cloistered Carmelite monastery in northern France. She never wrote a word of theology. And yet, Pope John Paul II declared St. Thérèse of Lisieux a doctor of the church. Ever wonder why?

Marie-Françoise-Thérèse Martin was the ninth and last child of a saintly couple. Her childhood was scarred with separations. She was four when her mother died. She later longed to follow her two eldest sisters to the Carmelite convent in Lisieux.

According to her spiritual autobiography, *The Story of a Soul*, her childhood came to a sudden end on Christmas Day, 1886. She rushed home from Midnight Mass knowing her shoes, placed in the chimney corner, would be filled with small gifts. As she climbed the steps to her bedroom, she overheard her father's justifiable comment that this would be the final year that Thérèse, nearly fourteen, would experience this childish custom.

She described this jolt as the "grace of leaving my childhood." In that instant, she says, she received the gift of "love and the spirit of self-forgetfulness." Thérèse's response to the cross was emerging.[1]

Path to Holiness

She joined her two sisters in the convent at age fifteen. Again she was the youngest, now among twenty-six other nuns. At her profession in September 1890, she took the name Sister Thérèse of the Infant Jesus and the Holy Face. Thérèse's holiness is found not in the convent's seven hours of daily prayer, nor in her domestic work, nor in her time in charge of the sacristy or as assistant to the mistress of novices. Her heroic sanctity is found in the way she performed her daily tasks even as she carried personal crosses. Attitude as everything. Her "Little Way," which evolved over the years, was the practical expression of her loving spirit of self-forgetfulness.

Her emotional suffering centered upon her father who, soon after she entered the convent, suffered a mental illness which necessitated a three-year institutionalization. Thérèse considered his illness her greatest suffering.

That suffering would be eclipsed on Good Friday, 1896, when she began exhibiting symptoms of tuberculosis. The twenty-three-year-old nun experienced incredible pain and bouts of suffocation. A few days later, she began experiencing a third cross, a complete loss of faith.

An incident of sheer desperation shows how she struggled to cling to God: Using her own tubercular blood which she had spit up, she penned the Apostles' Creed and pinned it to her religious habit.

Love Alone Counts

In the midst of all this, she continued to be faithful to the daily schedule, to give herself to community activities, and even to write devotional poems at the community's request. The attitude of self-forgetfulness consumed her.

When asked about her "Little Way" a few days before her death, Thérèse described it as the way of spiritual childhood, of confidence in and abandonment to God. Expressed in selfless deeds of love—a smile, a kind word, a simple act of charity—it was "to throw at Jesus' feet the flowers of little sacrifices, to win Him through our caresses."

The "Little Flower," as she once referred to herself, cared to give the very best—flowers symbolized in practical little sacrifices of self-forgetful love. The future doctor of the church summed up her secret the day before her death: "It is love alone that counts."

ST. JOHN OF THE CROSS *(1542–1591)*

Feast day: December 14

At age thirty-four, some members of his religious community felt so threatened by him that they imprisoned him in a small windowless room and routinely beat him three times a week. After nine months, he managed to escape under cover of night—making "night" an important symbol in his spiritual experience. Taking only the poetry he had composed during confinement, he climbed out a window and, over time, emerged as one of the greatest mystics of Christian spirituality. In 1926, he was named a doctor of the church.

Juan de Yepes y Álvarez was the youngest son of a wealthy silk merchant and a poor girl in Fontiveros, Spain. His father, disowned by his family for marrying below his rank, died soon after Juan's birth. His mother struggled to make ends meet, finally settling the homeless family in Medina del Campo.

After a basic education, John worked at the Plague Hospital de la Concepción. The hospital's founder offered the teenager the chance to attend a Jesuit school. Juan later turned down the opportunity to study for the diocesan priesthood. Instead, at age twenty, he entered the Carmelite Order and took the name John of St. Matthias. He continued his education and was ordained a priest in 1567.

An Agent of Reform

Returning to Medina del Campo to celebrate his first Mass, he met Teresa of Avila. This encounter would change his life as he agreed to bring her reform, based upon a stricter lifestyle of poverty and prayer, to the male Carmelite Order.

In November 1568, John and two other friars began to observe the primitive Carmelite Rule in a small farmhouse. Changing his name to John of the Cross, he led his followers in the practice of silence, prayer, and penance, together with a ministry of preaching and hearing confessions.

They wore coarse wool habits and went barefoot. Hence, they were called "Discalced" (shoeless) Carmelites in distinction to "Calced" (shoe-wearing) Carmelites.

John worked closely with Teresa in the reform. He followed her to the Convent of the Incarnation where she was superior. At the early age of thirty, he became the spiritual director to both Teresa and the entire convent.

In 1575, the Calced Carmelites began rejecting the reform. Soon after, John was imprisoned.

Poetry and the "Dark Night"

It was during this experience of the cross that John wrote his mystical poetry, which continues to inspire and encourage people in the life of prayer. After his escape under cover of night, some Carmelite nuns asked for an interpretation of his poetry. This led John to write some of his classic works: *The Ascent of Mount Carmel* and *The Dark Night of the Soul*; and explanations of the poem "Spiritual Canticle" as well as an untitled poem that begins, "O Living Flame of Love."

John is known for the concept of the "dark night of the soul." "Night" is the central symbol in his writings. It suggests that the spiritual journey is a mystery which challenges the believer to be led by blind faith in God. John used it to describe detachment, the active and deliberate renunciation of the possessive desire for anything. He also used it to describe the passive experience of the cross—the agony of depression, desolation, and the feeling of divine abandonment that God imposes on those whom God is leading to the deepest forms of contemplation.

Ill and unappreciated, John died at age forty-nine. Having accepted the cross both in name and in experience, he now enjoys endless light and eternal freedom.

St. Padre Pio (*1887–1968*)
Feast day: September 23

Padre Pio is a unique and polarizing figure. Known for his legendary ability to bilocate, he was also known for his good humor. When told that an airplane had traveled nonstop from Rome to New York in six hours, he quipped, "Good heavens, that is a long time! When I go, it takes me only a second." Padre Pio also bore the physical wounds of Christ in his body. Yet, at his canonization in 2002, no reference was made to his mystical gift for bilocation or to the stigmata. Rather, Pope John Paul II said in his homily, "The life and mission of Padre Pio prove that difficulties and sorrows, if accepted out of love, are transformed into a privileged way of holiness, which opens onto the horizons of a greater good, known only to the Lord."[2]

One of eight children, Francesco Forgione was born into a poor farming family in Pietrelcina, a small town in southern Italy. In the hopes of helping young Francesco pursue his call as a Capuchin priest, his father spent time in America and worked on the Long Island and Pennsylvania railroads.

Francesco entered the Capuchin order at age fifteen and was given the name Pio. Due to ill health he had to return home, where his pastor tutored him in philosophy and theology. In 1910, he was ordained a priest and became "Padre Pio."

Mystical Gift

On September 20, 1918, a year after arriving at the friary in San Giovanni Rotondo, Padre Pio, while praying, had a vision of Jesus. Afterward, he discovered quarter-sized holes in his hands and feet and a two-inch wound near his heart. He was able to hide the stigmata for a few days but, when the religious guardian of the friary ordered him to extend his hands, Padre Pio burst into tears of embarrassment. Life for him and his friary would never be the same.

Padre Pio lovingly accepted the consequences and inconveniences of this rare manifestation of the cross. Besides the physical pain it entailed, he endured the scrutiny of both medical science and the Vatican's Holy Office. In 1924 and again in 1931, the authenticity of the stigmata was questioned and major restrictions were placed on his ministry: He was not permitted to celebrate public Masses or to hear confessions for a period of time.

As word traveled about the stigmatist, hundreds of pilgrims made their way to Our Lady of Grace Friary. The life of the friary became centered upon the ministry of Padre Pio. He heard confessions ten to twelve hours a day. So many penitents came for confession that they were issued tickets. Added to his gift for hearing confessions were God's instant answers to his particular requests for healings and cures.

The Saving Cross

Padre Pio's spiritual life centered on Marian devotion and the recitation of the rosary, his public Masses (which could last up to three hours) and his daily fidelity to hearing confessions. But all of this flowed out of a heart surrendered to the cross. That was his secret. He once said, "If we knew the value of suffering, we would ask for nothing else." Clearly, he saw the redemptive and transformative quality of the cross.

Padre Pio's extraordinary compassion for those who suffered found expression not only in his ministry of prayer but also in what Pope Benedict XVI has called a "miracle": the construction of the House for the Relief of Suffering, still one of the largest, most modern hospitals in southern Italy. Conceived by the saint in 1940, its doors opened in 1956. Today, standing next to the friary of San Giovanni Rotondo, it holds over a thousand beds.

After being present for fifty years, the stigmata healed the week before his death. No doubt God was giving Padre Pio another gift—advance news of his resurrection.

STEPPING OUT IN FAITH

Turn your experiences of the cross into something life-giving. Follow in the footsteps of…

- St. Thérèse of Lisieux, whose spirit of self-forgetfulness helped her move beyond her own suffering to focus on God and others. Listen to the troubles of another without judgment or comparison to your own.
- St. John of the Cross, whose poetry and concept of the "dark night of the soul" have helped many on their spiritual journeys. Read a good book on the spiritual life, then share it with a friend.
- Padre Pio, whose compassion for those who suffer led him to build a hospital. Reach out to a friend, family member, or parishioner who is in the hospital or a nursing home. Commit to praying daily for the sick and suffering.

CHAPTER NINE

Martyrs: Belief in Action

Robert F. Morneau

Martyrs are witnesses of the faith. Their witness goes all the way; they are willing to lay down their lives for their religious convictions. Martyrs move beyond mere words into deeds, professing their beliefs in action. Manifesting a graced courage in the face of suffering and death itself, individuals like Sts. Agnes, Thomas More, Teresa Benedicta of the Cross (Edith Stein), Ignatius of Antioch, Archbishop Oscar Romero, and St. Stephen all participated in the self-giving of Jesus. We do well to reflect upon their lives and witness. Let us now ponder the faith unto death of Thomas Becket, Isaac Jogues, and Miguel Pro.

St. Thomas Becket *(1118–1170)*
Feast day: December 29

Religion and politics don't mix well. The church and the state have had a tumultuous relationship, one evidenced by considerable violence. In the twelfth century we see this conflict of church-state played out in the lives of Thomas Becket, archbishop of Canterbury, and Henry II, king of England. (Later, in the sixteenth century, a similar drama involved St. Thomas More and Henry VIII.)

At one time, Thomas Becket and Henry II were friends. Henry named Thomas his chancellor, the individual controlling the finances of the realm. When the Diocese of Canterbury opened, King Henry appointed Thomas Becket the new archbishop, though at the time Thomas was not even ordained a priest. After ordination and installation, he left behind his worldly ways and dedicated his life to being an authentic disciple of Jesus. This involved a renewed spiritual life and a decision to protect the church from encroachment by the state, namely, King Henry II.

Needless to say, the king was not pleased. Thomas was exiled to France for six years. From there he excommunicated the king and others when they transgressed privileges reserved to the religious leader of England. A reconciliation was attempted but failed. Thomas Becket eventually returned to England and then, on December 29, 1170, four of Henry II's knights entered the cathedral and killed the archbishop.

Finding a New Center

What happened in the mind and heart of Thomas Becket? As a friend and trusted companion of the king, what brought Thomas Becket to give up worldly power and influence to promote the gospel and the Kingdom? Surely, it was the action of grace. Becket said yes to friendship with God rather than friendship with a king who was going to exploit the church. Here is an example of a major conversion, a finding of a new center, and embarking on a whole new way of life.

Witness to the Truth

Thomas Becket was an ordinary person. God was always present to Becket, offering the gift of grace, namely, God's very life. At some moment, Becket said yes to that new life. Sainthood was not the result of doing "holy" things like extensive prayer and fasting; nor was it the product of pride or luck. Rather, it was the working of the Holy Spirit that empowered Becket to follow the path of truth, love, and courage.

Good or bad luck? Coincidence? Becket's life and death were part of God's providence. Perhaps in common speech we might say: "Becket was sure lucky to be given the gift of eternal life." But this simplifies the matter. God sends prophet, martyrs, and saints because the world needs witnesses to truth, beauty and goodness. Thomas Becket (and Thomas More) have influenced political leaders as well as common citizens to do the right thing regardless of the cost and sacrifice. The lives of the saints are not just good stories. They are narratives that challenge us to respond to God's call in our lives with courage and nobility.

St. Isaac Jogues (1607–1646)
Feast day: October 19
St. Isaac Jogues wanted everyone to know about the mystery of God revealed in Jesus. He left his native France and traveled to Quebec in North America. There he worked among the Hurons and Mohawks, communicating the good news of the gospel. He and his fellow Jesuits learned the language and customs of the Native Americans and grew to appreciate the spirituality already present among the various tribes. The Jesuits experienced what is known as reverse evangelization—an awareness that God has been at work in all times and all places long before any missionary approached a specific country or people. The challenge is to recognize how God's grace has been operative in that land and then to point out attitudes and behaviors that contradict gospel living.

Disciple of the Lord
While working with the Hurons and experiencing many hardships (cold, starvation, sickness), Isaac Jogues was captured by a warring party of Mohawks. He and his companions suffered brutal torture. Eventually, Isaac Jogues escaped and returned to France, where he was honored and acclaimed. His superiors allowed him to decide whether to remain in France or return to North America.

Return he did, in 1644. Two years later, while attempting to nego-tiate an agreement between the government of Quebec and the Mohawks, Jogues was martyred. He had left materials for the cele-bration of Mass in a Mohawk village. When an epidemic struck the village, the Mohawk people blamed these items for the disease and death. Upon his return to the village he was beaten and killed.

Jesus proclaims that anyone who leaves mother or father, brother or sister for the sake of the Kingdom will share in the joys of eter-nal life. Isaac Jogues left his beloved homeland and faced incredi-ble hardships to fulfill his vocation as a disciple of the Lord. Such sacrifice is admirable and worthy of emulation. Isaac Jogues did what Jesus did: He offered himself for the sake of the Kingdom.

Freedom and Grace

Isaac Jogues was a free man. Through grace he escaped the two prisons that incarcerate so many of us: self-regard and human respect. He had the liberty to do what God asked of him regardless of his own well-being or the opinion of others. Isaac Jogues referred everything to the Lord: the brutally cold winters, the cross of suf-fering, the joy of the Eucharist, and his preaching. United with Christ, all became holy.

As Isaac Jogues approached death he was not alone. The spirit of the Risen Lord filled his soul with courage and surely, like Jesus on the cross, the devoted missionary prayed for the forgiveness of those who killed him.

If we had been there we might have heard him saying under his breath: "Father, forgive them for they do not know what they are doing."

BLESSED MIGUEL PRO *(1891–1927)*

Feast day: November 23

Fr. Miguel Pro was involved in both political and personal revolutions. The political revolution was in Mexico, where violent repression of Catholicism was under way in the Revolution of 1910. Prior to being executed by a firing squad in November 1927, Fr. Pro performed his priestly ministry in disguise in Mexico City.

He managed to celebrate the sacraments, serve the needy and mediate God's courage and strength to those facing arrest and death. In 1988, Pope John Paul II beatified Miguel Pro as a martyr. Fr. Pro underwent a personal revolution. After studying in Europe, he returned to his native country and began his priestly work. During his years of formation, Miguel Pro learned to make God the center of his life.

This revolution is at the heart of conversion—the journey from self to God. It is a shifting of centers: God moves to the center, and we are on the periphery. Fr. Pro made that painful journey through God's transforming grace. Here was the source of his courage and endurance, the source of his holiness.

Revolutionary Trust

A significant part of Fr. Pro's personal conversion was how he dealt with his pain. The emotional suffering came from worrying about his family; his physical pain came from stomach problems. In the midst of these struggles, Fr. Pro trusted in God's providence as he would trust in God on the day he was executed. That trust was truly revolutionary.

Like St. Francis of Assisi, Fr. Pro trusted deeply in God's ways and God's will. The saint has eyes to see how God is manifest in all things and, because of that graced vision grounded in trust and faith, every person and event take on divine significance. St.

Francis, Miguel Pro, and all saints are individuals through whom the light, love, and life of grace are manifested. They become windows through which God shines.

The common people of Mexico responded to the death of Fr. Pro by acclaiming him a saint. The political machine that tried to eliminate the Catholic resistance had its plans turned upside down. The resistance only grew because of this martyr's blood. By proclaiming the good news of Jesus through his sacrificial death, Fr. Pro's witness to the gospel captured the imaginations and hearts of thousands of people.

Justice, Courage, the Cross
Long before the seven principles of Catholic social teaching were articulated, Fr. Pro was living them in his own unique way: He believed firmly in the dignity of every person, the call to solidarity, preferential option for the poor and vulnerable, rights and responsibilities. Just as the Mexican government of his day denied these values to the people, Fr. Miguel fought to protect and promote them. Blessed Miguel Pro was a man of justice and courage.

As he went before the firing squad on that fateful day in 1927, Fr. Pro extended his arms, making the form of a cross with his body before the bullets struck. This last gesture proclaimed the centrality of Jesus and the cross in the life of this saint. The true instrument of any graced revolution is this symbol from Calvary.

STEPPING OUT IN FAITH

Participate in the self-giving love of Jesus. Follow in the footsteps of…

- St. Thomas Becket, who said yes to friendship with God over friendship with the king. Recommit to your own friendship with God. Celebrate this with a friend who reveals God's love to you.
- St. Isaac Jogues, who faced hardships, torture, and death in order to bring the Good News to peoples of different cultures. Engage someone of a different ethnic background from yours in a conversation about the difference faith in God makes in your life.
- Blessed Miguel Pro, who trusted in God through both emotional and physical pain. Share your burdens with God. Reach out to others whose pain keeps them from reaching out to you. Listen as they share their pain without interjecting your own experiences.

| CHAPTER TEN |

Defenders of the Faith
Mitch Finley

The term "defender of the faith" may conjure up images of a stalwart figure clad in medieval armor bearing sword, buckler, and shield, setting forth Arthur-like to lower the boom of truth on those who would lead the faithful away from the true faith. In fact, the church understands the title defender of the faith in a broadminded way. It's a title conferred on individuals who are especially effective when it comes to representing what the Catholic faith is really all about. The three saints we will get to know better in this chapter certainly qualify.

St. Cyril of Alexandria *(c. 376–444)*
Feast day: June 27
Have you ever attended a funeral and heard the dearly departed eulogized as a good and virtuous person, yet you knew for a fact that he or she had more than a few human faults? Yes, she gave unselfishly to the poor…but she always made a big show of doing it. Yes, he was cheerful…but he regularly drank too much. And so forth.

Spend some time with those who lived with Blessed Mother Teresa of Calcutta for years, and you will eventually hear anecdotes not only about Mother Teresa's holiness and heroism, but also about her blind spots and lapses of patience. Even saints sometimes irritate other people, yet they become saints all the same.

Cyril of Alexandria is a good example of one such person. Cyril defended the truth tirelessly. He spoke up for the truth in public and he wrote lengthy treatises in opposition to well-meaning theological crackpots of his era. The very same Cyril, however, was a very difficult person to get along with. Indeed, he used his position as bishop of Alexandria to bully people, and it's even possible that, in the year 415, he had something to do with the murder of the philosopher Hypatia of Alexandria.

Defense of Christ's Identity

Still, Cyril became a saint and a doctor of the church by defending the Incarnation, one of the central doctrines of the Christian faith. The Incarnation is our belief that Jesus was both fully human and fully divine, and that neither nature overshadowed the other. Cyril did this not by writing about the Incarnation directly, but by insisting that Mary must be called the Mother of God (Greek, *theotokos*).

When the followers of a renegade bishop named Nestorius declared that it was wrong to call Mary the Mother of God, Cyril stood up at the Council of Ephesus in 431 and let go with the fifth-century Greek equivalent of, "Now, hold on just a darn minute there!" In our time, it would not be unusual to encounter people who do not believe that Jesus was—and now, in his risen state, is—both fully human and fully divine. Yet, since the time of St. Cyril of Alexandria, and especially since the Council of Chalcedon affirmed Cyril's teaching in 451, it has been the constant belief of the church that we must take in all seriousness both the divinity and humanity of Jesus.

Living the Faith

As believers today, we may find ourselves in situations where we, too, may speak up for the faith of the church. Some are even called to be apologists, defenders of the faith who explain its meaning through lectures, books, and articles.

An adult believer wants to have an adult understanding of the faith, and reading the occasional book about what it means to be Catholic is always worthwhile. But most of us will find ourselves called to "defend" our faith, above all and first of all, by living it. In doing so, we may attract the attention of believers and unbelievers alike, so that without our speaking a word about it they will notice our love for God and neighbor. That, in all times and all places— Cyril's time and place as well as our own time and place—is the best way to be a defender of the faith.

St. Philip Neri *(1515–1595)*
Feast day: May 26

Do you ever wonder what kind of world we're living in when it comes to religion and religious practice? It can seem that it's a religious smorgasbord out there, and people pick and choose whatever appeals to them based on subjective criteria alone, that is, whatever feels right. It may appear, too, that there is a great deal of apathy and indifference when it comes to religion, and that more than a few people resent any attempt to even bring up the topic of religion for discussion. Philip Neri lived in a very similar cultural environment, and he decided to do something about it. Philip was a young man on the way up. Born in Florence, Italy, Philip was one of four children of Francis Neri, a notary, who saw to it that Philip was given a first-rate education by the Dominicans. Philip's mother died when he was quite young, and he grew up a superficially pious boy who was popular with his peers.

At the age of eighteen, Philip was sent to San Marco to live with a bachelor relative who was a businessman. Philip's father hoped the relative would make Philip his heir. Soon after arriving, however, Philip had a profound experience which he referred to later as a "conversion." From then on, he had no wish to become a success in the eyes of the world.

Using His Gifts

Philip left for Rome with no money in his pocket and no plans, intending to rely entirely on the guidance of Divine Providence. When he arrived, he was taken in by a customs official, Galeotto Caccia, who gave him the job of tutoring his two young sons.

In return, Caccia gave Philip a modest room and simple food to eat. This arrangement suited the young man just fine.

After two years, during which Philip's spiritual life deepened and matured, he began to hang out on the street corners and in the marketplaces where he would engage all and sundry in conversation—in particular the young people who worked in the banks and shops. Using his gift of gab and his lively sense of humor, Philip gradually enticed many young people indifferent to religion to think about the love of God and to consider their relationship with Christ.

Rooted in Prayer and Community

In this way, his defense of the faith took the form of attracting lukewarm Catholics to a mature, adult practice of their faith. Note that Philip did this not by preaching or attempting to proselytize but by being of good cheer and by entering into cordial conversation. Late each evening, he would withdraw to a church or to the catacombs of St. Sebastian on the Appian Way, where he would turn his heart to Christ. On various occasions Philip had profound experiences of the love of God.

In 1548, when he was thirty-three, Philip sought and received the help of his confessor, Fr. Persiano Rossa, in organizing a fraternity of far-from-affluent laymen who would gather regularly for prayer and to care for poor pilgrims. Encouraged by Fr. Rossa to become a priest, Philip finally gave in and was ordained in 1551. Later, his informal group came to be called the Oratory, a fraternity of diocesan priests living in community.

In ways that made sense for his time and place, St. Philip Neri defended the faith against religious apathy and, using the gifts he had been given, proclaimed the gospel and lived it in ways that changed people's hearts.

St. Vincent Ferrer *(c. 1350–1419)*
Feast day: April 5

It is possible to have a theological conviction that turns out to be completely wrong, yet still become a saint. Vincent Ferrer is a classic example.

Vincent Ferrer's early life was noteworthy because he joined the Dominicans when he was only fifteen; in addition, he was highly gifted intellectually. In fact, at the age of twenty-one he taught philosophy at the University of Lérida, in Spain, even before his own education was complete. When he was twenty-nine, Vincent was ordained a priest and became a member of the court of Cardinal Pedro de Luna.

The year before that, Cardinal de Luna had helped elect Pope Urban VI, but later de Luna became convinced that this election had been invalid. He then joined a group of cardinals who proceeded to elect another man as Pope Clement VII. This second election resulted in the famous schism that led to several popes residing in Avignon, France, over some decades. Then, in 1394, de Luna himself was elected to succeed Clement VII. He took the name Benedict XIII. Vincent Ferrer honestly believed that the Avignon popes were the legitimate heirs to the chair of St. Peter. He became an ardent champion of the Avignon papacy. He was also reported to the Inquisition for heresy because he taught that Judas, the betrayer of Jesus, had later repented of his sin.

His friend Pedro de Luna, who was now the antipope Benedict, dismissed the charge, however, and made Vincent a member of his court. Subsequently, Vincent became a celebrated traveling preacher.

A Change of Heart

In 1408, however, while ministering in plague-stricken Genoa, Vincent became concerned about the impact of the Avignon papacy on the unity of the church. He tried to talk his old friend Benedict into withdrawing his claim to the papacy, but Benedict would have no part of that. One day, wearied by the whole situation, Vincent let Benedict have it with both barrels (verbally, from the pulpit) when Benedict was present in church together with a huge assembly.

After this public chastising by Vincent, all of Benedict's followers abandoned him, and Benedict fled Avignon. Soon thereafter, in 1414 at the Council of Constance, unity was restored to the church. A French statesman and writer named Gerson remarked to Vincent Ferrer, "But for you, this union could never have been achieved."

Five years later, following an exhausting preaching tour in France, Vincent Ferrer died in Brittany at about the age of seventy. Thirty-six years later, he was canonized, in no small part because of his role in helping to restore the unity of the church.

Unity as a Value

St. Vincent Ferrer teaches us that there are values that transcend religious disagreements. In Vincent's case the value was the unity of the church, which he came to see as far more important than arguing over who was the legitimate pope. This is an issue not without relevance in our own time when splinter Catholic groups claim that the last legitimate pope was Pius XII (1939–1958), and that the election of his successor, Pope John XXIII, was invalid. This means that, for these groups, the Second Vatican Council, called by Pope John, was also invalid.

But Vincent's example also has more personal applications. Whenever we have an opinion about some spiritual or theological issue, about some issue in parish life or about anything having to do with the church, we may well ask ourselves if there are not values of more importance for which we should be willing to set aside differences of opinion about lesser matters.

STEPPING OUT IN FAITH

Defend your faith by really living it. Follow in the footsteps of...

- St. Cyril of Alexandria, who spoke the truth in spite of opposition. What truth or truths of our faith are you called to defend or explain? Don't ever be afraid to speak up for the truth. Christian discipleship isn't about popularity.
- St. Philip Neri, who used his gift of gab and sense of humor to attract lukewarm Catholics to deeper faith. Use your own gifts to reach out to those in your family, circle of friends, or parish who have become distant from the church.
- St. Vincent Ferrer, whose humility allowed him to change his mind in the interest of church unity. Initiate conversation with someone who holds a different position than you do on a church issue.

| CHAPTER ELEVEN |

Immigrant Saints: Newcomers to the Americas
Vicky Hébert and Denis Sabourin

What relevance do the stories of a German priest and two nuns—one Italian, the other French, all immigrants—have for us living today? These pioneers crossed an ocean to work in the mission territory of the United States for the welfare of immigrants, elevating the importance of parochial education, building schools and churches, and working to re-instill Catholic family virtues in the New World. The recounting of the obstacles these role models faced reads like a page from today's news. Their struggle is our own.

St. Frances Xavier Cabrini *(1850–1917)*
Feast day: November 13

Mother Cabrini was cut from a different cloth. She saw a problem and worked to solve it. The youngest in a family of thirteen, Maria Francesca was born in Sant'Angelo, Italy, in 1850. A delicate, obedient, shy, hard-working child, she was precociously devout. Her dearest dream was to join the religious order that educated her and, as a teacher, to be a missionary in the Far East. However, due to her small stature and presumed delicate health, she was repeatedly refused admission. Still, her resolve did not wane.

After Maria had made several requests to her bishop, he encouraged her to establish her own order of missionary sisters. After serving at a small orphanage, she founded the Missionary Sisters of the

Sacred Heart. The motto of the new congregation, "I can do all things through him who strengthens me," speaks volumes about her heroic trust in God.

Missionary Zeal

In the seven years that followed, she and her sisters—with little or no means—founded missions, schools, and hospitals. Now known as Mother Frances Xavier, later as Mother Cabrini, she went to Rome to meet Pope Leo XIII, from whom she secured solid financial backing as well as his personal approval. The pope offered her the opportunity to fulfill her dream of becoming a missionary to a far-off land. He asked her to take her sisters to the United States to help the large numbers of Italian immigrants. These poor souls had left their homeland under the promise of a better life, only to find themselves in dire straits. Unable to speak the local language, they faced prejudice, fell victim to exploitation and were forced to live in overcrowded, disease-ridden tenements that became known as "Little Italies." These people needed direction. They needed hope. They needed a miracle!

Upon arriving in New York City, Mother Cabrini was astonished when the accommodations and school she had been promised never materialized. Her embarrassed host, Archbishop Corrigan, even suggested that she and her companions return to Italy. But she was in the United States to stay.

Graced with phenomenal administrative abilities, she founded sixty-seven institutions, all devoted to caring for children, the ill and those who live a marginalized existence. Houses were founded in Central and South America and Europe as well. Despite all manner of opposition and even the destruction of her convents in Central America through two revolutions, Mother Cabrini never gave up.

Courageous Faith

Why do we want to know about this woman and her work? Her story is an epic of hope; she is an encouraging saint in a time when people need encouragement. Mother Cabrini, who made over thirty ocean crossings yet never learned to swim, was desperately frightened of the water! Similar stories abound of her courageous voyages to help those in need. She believed that one served God by helping God's people, especially children. In an act of faith and patriotic love, at the age of fifty-nine, Mother Cabrini became a United States citizen.

On December 22, 1917, Mother Frances Xavier Cabrini, in her own Columbus Hospital in Chicago, died of pneumonia brought on by a recurrence of malaria. She was canonized in 1946.

St. Frances Xavier Cabrini is the first United States citizen to become a saint. In 1950, she was designated patroness of all immigrants.

ST. JOHN NEUMANN *(1811–1860)*
Feast day: January 5

What is a young seminarian to do when, after years of preparation, the time comes for ordination and the bishop refuses, stating, "Not this year! We already have more priests than we need. Try to find a congregation that is looking for priests." This was exactly the case for John Nepomucene Neumann.

Born in 1811 to Czech-German parents, John was a quiet, serious student who discovered the need for missionary priests to help new immigrants, mostly German-speaking, in the United States. John left his home diocese and walked most of the way to Le Havre in France—a distance of some nine hundred miles—where he boarded ship for a forty-day voyage across the Atlantic.

Arriving unannounced in Manhattan in June 1836, John presented himself to the local bishop, who ordained him without delay. Immediately sent to Buffalo, New York, John relished his new responsibilities—caring for the spiritual needs of the rural folk. Traveling by foot, he left to visit the members of his widely dispersed flock, ready to discuss their spiritual needs in any of the twelve languages he spoke fluently. People welcomed him into their homes.

For the Good of Society

For four years, John Neumann witnessed the devotional work done among the immigrants by the Redemptorist Fathers. He came to believe that he could be more effective as a member of this religious order than as a solitary missionary priest. Fr. John Neumann became the first novice for the Redemptorists in America and, later, the first American in the congregation to profess final vows. A bishop by the age of just forty-one—a position he reluctantly accepted—he expressed his deep love for the United States by becoming an American citizen in 1848. The "Little Bishop," as he was affectionately called, left a lasting legacy. He founded fifty churches, instituted the Forty Hours devotion, and fully mapped out a plan for Catholic education, establishing a hundred schools in the United States. He was also a prolific writer.

John Neumann's personal mission statement provided the motivation for his tireless work:

> [A]ll people of whatever race, condition or age, in virtue of their dignity as human persons, have an inalienable right to education...suitable to their destiny, adapted to their abilities, sex and national cultural traditions...conducive to amicable relations with other nations to promote true unity and peace in the world...directed towards...the good of society...[where] as adults, they will have their share of duties to perform.[1]

Immigrant Shepherd

What can we take from the example provided by the short life of John Neumann? He worked to help those who could not help themselves. He brought spirituality to the new immigrants. He brought hope and the melody of a familiar language, all the while shoring up the foundations of the church in the New World. As he visited the immigrants in their own homes, speaking to them in their own language, he encouraged trust that only the familiarity of a country-man can invite.

At the time of his sudden fatal collapse at the age of forty-nine, his confreres were reminded of one of his final remarks: "A person must always be ready, for death comes when and where God wills it." John Neumann was the first American bishop to be beatified (in 1963) and then canonized (in 1977). Referred to as "the immigrant shepherd," John Neumann is considered the patron saint of the United States of America.

ST. THÉODORE GUÉRIN *(1798–1856)*
Feast day: October 3
Canonized in October 2006, Mother Théodore Guérin was a woman of uncommon courage and intelligence. She lived a life of extraor-dinary virtue in the most difficult of settings: the New World. A nat-urally gifted teacher, she founded a new religious congregation, the Sisters of Providence of Saint Mary-of-the-Woods. She also founded the first Catholic women's college in the United States.

Anne-Thérèse Guérin was born in Étables, Brittany (France) in 1798, the daughter of one of Napoleon's naval lieutenants. She was twenty-five years old when she finally received her widowed mother's consent to join the Sisters of Providence of Ruillé-sur-Loire. Taking the name Sister Théodore, she spent eight years in France administering schools, teaching, opening day care centers, and even acting as a business agent for her order. During the follow-ing six years she took the opportunity to study pharmacy and med-icine with a local doctor.

Trust and Hope
At this time in the United States, new immigrants were heading west in search of prairies and pasture lands. One of her country-men, the first bishop of Vincennes in Indiana (now part of the

Archdiocese of Indianapolis), needed the help of a religious congregation to minister to his largely French-speaking parishioners. (At that time, the archdiocese stretched across the entire state of Indiana and included the eastern third of Illinois.)

The mother superior at the Ruillé congregation suggested that Sister Théodore, with five other sisters, would be ideal. She would be superior general of the United States order. Sister Théodore's advisor, the Bishop of Le Mans, wrote, when asked his advice: "The Lord did not choose the powerful for His Apostles.... He chose humble working people..." The bishop advised that she should prepare for the worst but pray for the best, always trusting in the Lord. Following his advice, the six sisters set sail in July 1840.

Two months later, they landed in New York City, where Sister Théodore remarked, "The true country for a Christian...is heaven." Their seemingly endless journey saw them travel overland by various means, arriving at their mission near Terre Haute, Indiana, in a deeply forested area called Saint Mary-of-the-Woods. Beset by various setbacks, Mother Guérin, as she was now known, trusted in divine providence as she knelt to pray for the first time in their poor log chapel. Immediately infused with a sudden overflowing of grace, she felt something inexplicable: hope.

Model of Christian Love
Less than a year after the Sisters' arrival, they opened Saint Mary's Academy for Young Ladies in July 1841; it later became Saint Mary-of-the-Woods College. Although Mother Théodore taught the students in the manner of the French school system, she stressed not only religion but patriotism as well. Students had to learn the history of the United States and its great leaders.

Mother Guérin and her Sisters of Providence established schools in more than a dozen places in Indiana and others in Illinois. Vincennes saw an orphanage opened for boys and one for girls.

Mother worked to open pharmacies where medicine was dispensed free to the poor at both Vincennes and Saint Mary-of-the-Woods.

Plagued by uncertain health most of her adult life, Mother Théodore Guérin died on May 14, 1856. A model of Christian love, she overcame many challenges and persevered in the Lord's work. Her cause, opened in 1908, came to fruition with her beatification in 1998 and canonization eight years later.

STEPPING OUT IN FAITH
Leave the familiarity of home to share faith with others. Follow in the footsteps of…

- St. Frances Xavier Cabrini, who made many ocean crossings in spite of her fear of water and inability to swim. Explore your own fears and the ways they inhibit your growth as a disciple. Trust God to lead you.
- St. John Neumann, who put his feet to the pavement in order to become a priest in the New World and in his ministry to his widespread flock. Commit yourself to a new path of service.
- St. Théodore Guérin, who clung to hope in discouraging situations and persevered to help educate and tend to the needs of others. Reach out to someone who is discouraged and offer him or her the hope that comes with another's care and concern.

| CHAPTER TWELVE |

Saints of the Twentieth Century
Robert F. Morneau

Three saints of the twentieth century were special bearers of God's light, love, and life: Katharine Drexel, Maximilian Kolbe, and Faustina Kowalska. They, as all saints, received God's grace and transmitted that life to those they met. Sainthood is as simple as that: receiving and sharing God's incredible love, light, and life. Pope Paul VI maintained that the two great needs for the church and the world are mentors and models, teachers, and witnesses. Saints teach us by sharing their wisdom; saints guide us by living the gospel in heroic ways. Through baptism, all of us are called to be mentors and models for others.

ST. KATHARINE DREXEL *(1858–1955)*
Feast day: March 3
In her book *Saint-Watching*, Phyllis McGinley wrote:

> When I was seven years old I wanted to be a tight-rope dancer and broke my collar bone practicing on a child's-size high wire. At twelve I planned to become an international spy. At fifteen my ambition was the stage. Now in my sensible or declining years I would give anything (except my comforts, my customs, and my sins) to be a saint.[1]

What Katharine Drexel wanted to be at age seven or twelve, we do not know. But that she eventually wanted to be a saint, of that we can be assured. Her life was one of generosity and service, of commitment and love. It was a life rooted in Jesus, especially in devotion to the Blessed Sacrament. It was a life that bore abundant fruits because of her spirit of tremendous sacrifice.

Minding the Margins
Katharine Drexel's ambition was not for the stage but for helping two groups of people who were marginalized from our culture: Native Americans and blacks.

The daughter of a wealthy Philadelphia banker who had left her and her siblings an inheritance in the millions, Katharine used her portion to establish Xavier University, the first Catholic college for blacks, in New Orleans. Her assistance to Native Americans resulted in one hundred and forty-five Catholic missions and twelve schools. Over the years, twelve million dollars from the Drexel estate went to this missionary activity.

This twentieth-century saint, who was canonized by Pope John Paul II in 2000, is a model for our twenty-first century. Just as St. Katharine responded to the diversity in the culture of her day, we are challenged today to reach out to the immigrants and refugees looking for a home. So many of the residents in our country are on the margins, struggling to find work and shelter and safety. So many of those who live in our culture face discrimination and intolerance. And we need not only individuals and communities, like St. Katharine and the community she founded, the Sisters of the Blessed Sacrament. We also need to change systems that deny people basic human rights.

Giving Up Much to Do More
The ministry to the Native Americans and blacks that Katharine Drexel began must continue to be a major concern as we respond to the call for a new evangelization. In our day, the Good News

of God's love and mercy in Jesus needs dedicated witnesses—individuals as committed as the heiress who gave away her wealth, her energy, her very life. In 1878, when Katharine Drexel asked Pope Leo XIII to assist her work with Native Americans, the pope told her to become a missionary herself. And she did!

Two virtues are evident in the life of Katharine Drexel, as they are in the lives of all saints. One is obedience, that graced listening to God's will. The second is self-giving, that costly sacrifice of one's life for others. These virtues characterize the life of a eucharistic person, one who through the Liturgy of the Word hears God's call, and through the Offertory, Consecration and Communion of the Mass, participates in the self-giving of Jesus. St. Katharine was such a eucharistic person.

Phyllis McGinley thought about being a tight-rope dancer, an international spy, an actress. Katharine Drexel probably had her daydreams and fantasies growing up, but in the end she gave up her comforts, her customs, and her sins to be a disciple of Jesus. She said yes to what God asked of her. That's all a saint has to do.

St. Maximilian Kolbe *(1894–1941)*

Feast day: August 14

Even in the darkest of times, God's light keeps breaking forth. In the darkness of the Second World War, a time of incredible suffering and human anguish, a light broke forth through a Franciscan priest named Maximilian Kolbe. He gave his life so that another man might be spared and eventually return to his wife and children.

The story is poignant. Ten prisoners in the concentration camp in Auschwitz were chosen at random to die because a fellow prisoner had escaped. One of the ten, Francis Gajowniczek, was a husband and parent. When Fr. Kolbe heard of the man's plight, he volunteered to take Gajowniczek's place. Eventually, all ten individuals died, Fr. Kolbe and three others by means of lethal injections. The date was August 14, 1941.

This bare outline says something of the heroic charity and graced courage of Maximilian Kolbe. We must pause to ponder how similar Kolbe's love is to that of Jesus. Both gave their very lives for another; both made manifest the fortitude that says that faith is stronger than death. Saints are individuals who are willing to sacrifice all; saints are individuals who do not allow fear to govern their destiny.

Model of Selfless Love
Maximilian Kolbe was born in Poland in 1894. He became a Franciscan at age sixteen. Early on, he knew sickness (tuberculosis) and the meaning of suffering. His devotion to Mary was strong and traditional. His zeal drew many others into an appreciation of the role of Mary in the Christian story. Surely it was Mary's obedience to God's word and her giving of self that prepared Kolbe to eventually follow her example. Maximilian was obedient and self-giving, the essence of discipleship and sanctity.

In 1982, Pope John Paul II canonized his fellow Pole in Rome. Francis Gajowniczek, the husband and father for whom Fr. Kolbe gave his life, was present at the ceremony. Forty-one years after the supreme act of love and courage was made, a saint-martyr was officially recognized.

Sharing the Light
In his classic work *The Varieties of Religious Experience: A Study of Human Nature*, William James captures much of what sainthood is all about:

> The saints, with their extravagance of human tenderness, are the great torch-bearers of this belief [the sacredness of every individual], the tip of the wedge, the clearers of the darkness. Like the single drops which sparkle in the sun they are flung far ahead of the advancing edge of a wave-crest or of a flood, they show the way and are forerunners.

The world is not yet with them, so they often seem in the midst of the world's affairs to be preposterous. Yet they are impregnators of the world, vivifiers and animators of potentialities of goodness which but for them would lie for-ever dormant. It is not possible to be quite as mean as we naturally are, when they have passed before us. One fire kindles another; and without that overtrust in human worth which they show, the rest of us would lie in spiritual stagnancy.[2]

St. Maximilian Kolbe, priest and martyr, is a "clearer of darkness" and a bearer of God's love. Although few of us will ever be in cir-cumstances similar to those that Fr. Kolbe had to face, all of us are called to bear God's love and be agents of God's light. Our vocation is essentially the same: to be recipients and transmitters of grace. St. Maximilian did this in a heroic way; we will be asked to do this in more humble circumstances. But in the end it is all for the glory of God and the salvation of the world.

St. Maria Faustina Kowalska *(1905–1938)*
Feast day: October 5

On April 30, 2000, Pope John Paul II canonized Maria Faustina Kowalska, a Polish nun and mystic. Seven years earlier, Faustina had been beatified and recognized as a woman outstanding in holi-ness and for her dedication to God's mercy revealed in Jesus. Although she died at age thirty-three, her influence has been tremendous. One of the influences has been the publication of her diary, *Divine Mercy in My Soul: The Diary of St. Faustina.*

In this diary, she records her inner experiences of Jesus and of the Blessed Virgin Mary. For some time the diary was misinter-preted and even questioned for its orthodoxy. But when Pope John Paul II came upon the scene, Faustina was vindicated, and her writ-ings were presented as worthy of study and prayerful reflection.

Speaking of God's Mercy

Another influence of St. Faustina is liturgical. The Second Sunday of Easter has been designated as Divine Mercy Sunday. Now the universal church has been asked to ponder the mystery of our merciful God. How fitting that this celebration is given to our world.

In *Secularity and the Gospel: Being Missionaries to Our Children*, Fr. Ronald Rolheiser writes: "In a world and a culture that is full of wounds, anger, injustice, inequality, historical privilege, jealousy, resentment, bitterness, murder, and war, we must speak always and everywhere about forgiveness, reconciliation, and God's healing."[3] Indeed, of God's *mercy!*

The third of ten Kowalska children, Maria Faustina experienced wounds, jealousy, resentment, and much more: Her parents tried to prevent her from entering religious life; as a religious, she was often ridiculed for her claim of seeing Christ; she was not of robust health and contracted tuberculosis, which lead to her early death. In others words, Faustina participated in the sufferings of Christ and understood from the inside the transforming power of love and mercy.

Confidence in God's Goodness

It is interesting that another religious and mystic, St. Thérèse of Lisieux (1873–1897), now a doctor of the church, would also write an autobiography, *The Story of a Soul*, in which she would say that her God was a God of Love and Mercy. Again and again, we find the great saints confirming one another's experience and driving home the point that our God is total self-gift.

And just as St. Thérèse, the Little Flower, claimed that her mission of doing good on earth would continue in heaven, so St. Faustina would write: "I feel certain that my mission will not come to an end upon my death, but will begin. O doubting souls, I will draw aside for you the veils of heaven to convince you of God's goodness."[4]

Another doctor of the church, St. Bernard, wrote: "The prophet does not exempt himself from the general wretchedness, lest he be left out of the mercy too." Maria Faustina Kowalska was keenly aware of her own unworthiness, but she was even more keenly aware of God's mercy. She was open to this grace and devoted herself to helping others experience God's merciful love.

Our twenty-first century is in special need of the grace of mercy. We are a blaming society, seeking again and again to assign guilt and responsibility in an undue fashion. True, we are free and responsible to a large extent. But it is equally true that we are weak and limited creatures, in need of forgiveness and mercy. St. Faustina knew this and will intercede for all of us to be open to this grace.

STEPPING OUT IN FAITH

Bring God's light, love and life to your corner of the world! Follow in the footsteps of…

- St. Katharine Drexel, who responded to the diversity in her culture with generosity and a spirit of sacrifice. Initiate a conversation about diversity and prejudice within your community. Commit to action that promotes the dignity of all God's children.
- St. Maximilian Kolbe, who cleared the darkness of death and despair by sacrificing his life for another. What darkness can you help clear by your own acts of sacrifice?
- St. Maria Faustina Kowalska, who was devoted to helping others experience God's merciful love. Where are you being called to share God's mercy and love? Who in your family most needs to experience the compassion, healing, and freedom offered by God? What can you do to bring this about?

FREQUENTLY ASKED QUESTIONS

Q: Why are there so many more male than female saints and blesseds?

A: In the worldwide liturgical calendars for January and May 2007, there are twelve men and two women for each month (counting saints and blesseds but not counting feasts of Mary). In general, more male than female martyrs are recognized individually. In male-dominated societies, executing male leaders was meant to discourage anyone from being a Christian. There were, in fact, many women martyrs.

The twelve apostles and ten popes are honored individually. Since 1970, three women have joined the thirty men as doctors of the church. Saints canonized by John Paul II between 2000 and 2005 include twenty-two women and twenty men, not counting all one hundred and twenty members of the Chinese martyrs.

Q: What does the church teach about Mary Magdalene?

A: Many Catholics mistakenly link Mary Magdalene with the "sinful woman" who washed Jesus' feet with her tears (see Luke 7:36–50). Even though Pope Gregory the Great (590–604) said that they were, they are not the same person. The Gospels affirm that Mary Magdalene was the first person to see the empty tomb on Easter Sunday. She was called the "apostle to the apostles" for proclaiming that fact.

Q: What are the names of the Eastern Catholic Churches and who are some of the saints they venerate?

A: There are twenty-one Eastern Catholic Churches. According to the statistics in the 2007 Official Catholic Directory, the five largest in the United States are, in descending order, the Chaldean, Byzantine, Syro-Malabar, Maronite, and Ukrainian Churches.

Besides venerating Mary, the apostles, other New Testament saints, martyrs, and confessors, these churches hold in special honor saints such as Gregory the Illuminator (d. 300, patron of Armenia), Irene of Thessalonika (d. 304, martyr), Pachomius (d. 346, founder of Egyptian monasticism), and Macrina the Younger (d. 379, monastic foundress).

Various Eastern Churches also highly respect, for example, Maro of Cyr (d. 423, Syrian monk and spiritual father of the Maronites), Melania the Younger (d. 439, nun in Bethlehem) and Andrei Rublev (d. 1430, iconographer).

In May 2000, Pope John Paul II joined Orthodox, Anglican, and Protestant leaders at the Colosseum in Rome for an ecumenical commemoration of twentieth-century witnesses to the faith. Three Orthodox and two Eastern Catholics were among the sixteen people identified by name, representing thousands of uncanonized people.

Q: Religious orders and congregations have certain charisms. What is a charism, and how does it become associated with a religious community?

A: The word *charism* comes from the Greek word for gift. St. Paul speaks of charisms as building up the Body of Christ, the church (1 Corinthians 12:1–14:40). As applied to a religious order or congregation, it means the way in which this group seeks to be a gift to the church—through its works but especially through the witness of its life.

Vatican II's "Decree on the Adaptation and Renewal of Religious Life" states: "redounds to the good of the Church that institutes have their own particular characteristics and work. Therefore let their founders' spirit and special aims they set before them as well as their sound traditions—all of which make up the patrimony of each institute—be faithfully held in honor." (#2).[1]

Benedictines and Jesuits, for example, have distinct charisms. Many Benedictines tend to stay in the monastery where they joined, praying the Liturgy of the Hours in common, engaging in the monastery's apostolates and offering hospitality to retreatants and other visitors.

Most Jesuits are involved in educational institutions, the missions or in some specialized ministry. Their life demands a flexibility that is incompatible with the monastic life. Both charisms build up the church.

Q: Were there saints who disagreed with each other or who didn't always get along?

A: Yes, there were. Sts. Paul and Barnabas disagreed over whether John-Mark should accompany them on their second missionary journey (see Acts 15:36–40). Paul went with Silas, and Barnabas traveled with John-Mark.

At a general audience last January, Pope Benedict referred to this incident and said, "There are also disputes, disagreements and controversies among saints. And I find this very comforting, because we see that the saints have not 'fallen from heaven.' They are people like us, who also have complicated problems." He went on to say that our capacity for reconciliation and forgiveness makes us saints.

See Galatians 2:11–14 for St. Paul's description of a major disagreement he had with St. Peter over how Jewish Christians and gentile Christians should relate. Sts. Jerome and Augustine are both doctors of the church, but they sometimes disagreed sharply. Sts. Cyprian and Cornelius differed about whether the church could forgive Christians who denied the faith during persecution but wanted to be reconciled during peaceful times.

Disagreements can be obstacles in the road or they can even end a common journey. Saints stress their common sharing in God's life of grace and go on.

Q: When did the church begin canonizing saints? Who is the first saint to be canonized formally? How were especially holy people recognized before the process was formalized?

A: Local bishops recognized holy people long before 993, the year that Pope John XV canonized Bishop Udalricus (Ulrich) of Augsburg, who lived 890–973. This was the first papal canonization for someone who had lived outside the Diocese of Rome. Like other bishops, the pope had been canonizing local people for centuries.

Local bishops continued to canonize people until 1234, when Pope Gregory IX decreed that because saints pertain to the entire church, only the Bishop of Rome may canonize a person.

In fact, the Roman Canon of the Mass, which was finalized in the fifth century and is now known as Eucharistic Prayer I, listed forty saints until Blessed John XXIII added St. Joseph in 1962. Most of the Roman Canon's saints were apostles or had a connection to the Eternal City.

Kenneth Woodward's 1996 book, *Making Saints: How the Catholic Church Determines Who Becomes a Saint, Who Doesn't and Why*, is a gold mine of information about how the saint-making process has evolved over the centuries.

It is God who makes saints. The church formally recognizes what God has already done.

Q: Why are there so few married saints? Some widows or widowers have established religious communities and were later canonized, but are there any couples who are saints precisely as married people?

A: There are certainly couples who were martyred for their faith, but the Catholic Church's worldwide liturgical calendar includes only one couple canonized for living their married vocation well—Isidore and Maria, whose feast is May 15.

That makes the Feast of All Saints (November 1) even more important because most people now in heaven were not lifelong celibates or people who took a vow of celibacy after once being married.

Dioceses have been encouraged to propose couples and have done so, but this involves proving the holiness of two people, not one. Most women and men now formally recognized as saints have been promoted by a religious community or by a diocese.

Canonizations are not a favor that the church does for God but are a formal recognition of people who have already generously cooperated with God's grace. They are a favor that the church does for itself.

In that sense, the current imbalance suggests that marriage is not a vocation likely to lead to holiness. Our experience suggests otherwise. In his book *Married Saints*, John Fink describes two dozen married saints and their conjugal path to holiness.

Q: Which saints have received the stigmata, the wounds of Jesus Christ? What is the relevance of this unusual gift?
A: I cannot give a definitive list. Francis of Assisi (1182–1226) is considered by some to be the church's first stigmatic. Padre Pio of Pietrelcina (1887–1968), who was canonized in 2002, is perhaps the most famous modern stigmatic.

In his book *Making Saints*, Kenneth Woodward reports that one list identifies three hundred twenty-five full or partial stigmatics since the thirteenth century. Only sixty-two of them have been canonized.

Being a stigmatic gives no assurance of being canonized a saint; rather, it emphasizes a person's generous cooperation with God's grace. Receiving the stigmata is a one-time event; responding to God's grace is ongoing.

Q: Is it only through suffering that saints have mystical experiences?

A: Mystics are women and men who see clearly and feel intensely the oneness of God's creation and ongoing action. Suffering might be part of that insight, but a person in perfect health could also be a mystic. Sts. Teresa of Avila and Teresa Benedicta of the Cross (Edith Stein) were certainly mystics, but their sufferings did not guarantee that. The same is true of Sts. Bernard of Citeaux and John of the Cross.

Not all mystics are Christians, but all mystics have a very strong sense of God's providence and of their need to make good decisions.

Q: Why are so many of the saints martyrs? Are there modern martyrs who are on the path to canonization?

A: Martyrs dominated the lists of saints in the church's earliest years because during the Roman persecutions they paid the ultimate price for believing in Jesus Christ.

Pope John Paul II canonized individual modern martyrs, such as Edith Stein, plus groups of martyrs from Korea, Japan, Vietnam, Paraguay, Slovakia, Spain, Mexico, and China.

He also beatified numerous martyrs, some of whom may be declared saints one day at Rome's Colosseum on May 7, 2000, Pope John Paul II joined with Orthodox, Anglican, Lutheran, Methodist, Pentecostal, Moravian, and other Christian leaders to commemorate twentieth-century witnesses of faith. Most of them were martyrs like Trappist Father Christian de Chergé, who died in Algeria in 1996.

Q: Is it OK to pray to the saints for assistance (for example, healing, or guidance) or should we simply ask them to pray for us and with us?

A: Yes, we should pray to the saints—not as an attempt to do an end-run around God but to enlist them as special friends who can obtain what our prayers alone cannot do. The saints point us to God and encourage us to cooperate generously with God's grace in every circumstance, as they did.

Q: Some people say that having a statue or picture of a saint is idolatry, a violation of the First Commandment. Is that true?

A: Already in the eighth century, so-called iconoclasts justified destroying icons of saints as a way of avoiding idolatry. At the Second Council of Nicaea (787), church leaders adopted the terminology of worship (*latria*, "for God alone") and veneration (*doulia*, "for saints"). A special category for venerating Mary (*hyperdoulia*) was recognized.

Catholics and other Christians do not worship Mary and the saints. Contemporary believers recognize them as outstanding examples of people who cooperated generously with God's grace and who invite us to do the same.

A statue of Mary or any other saint has no significance or power apart from God, to whom the saints always point believers.

Q: What about lighting candles in front of a statue or picture? Or wearing a medal with a saint's image?

A: This is permissible because we are honoring the person, not the object itself. The saint shows us one way of cooperating generously with God's grace—for example, as a teacher, a parent, a champion of the poor. Idolatry invests physical objects with their own power. The prophet Isaiah ridiculed pagans who had to carry their idols to safety during wars (46:1–7).

Q: Does the church require or simply encourage giving a child a saint's name at baptism and confirmation? Is there a complete list of saints' names available?

A: According to Canon 855 of the 1983 *Code of Canon Law*, which applies only to the Latin-Western Church, the name must not be "foreign to Christian sentiment." The 1917 Code had indicated that the newly baptized person was to be given a Christian name or that a saint's name should be added to the person's name.

The name *Satan* would clearly be "foreign to Christian sentiment," as the Canon Law Society of Great Britain and Ireland notes in *The Canon Law: Letter and Spirit: A Practical Guide to the Code of Canon Law.* The custom of giving a saint's name is a way of indicating that following Jesus is possible in every time and place. The *Martyrologium Romanum* lists the names of over eight thousand saints. Many Catholic publishers have books listing saints' names.

Q: How are patron saints assigned?
A: In 1927, Pope Pius XI designated Sts. Francis Xavier and Thérèse of Lisieux as co-patrons of the missions. Most patrons, however, arise from ordinary people who link some saint to a particular place, occupation or activity.

Q: What is the difference between beatification and canonization?
A: The difference is in how widespread the person's feast can be celebrated liturgically. Saints are not more "in heaven" than blesseds are. Saints are simply recognized for veneration by the entire church, whereas a blessed is recognized for veneration by a particular group or region within the church.

When Padre Pio of Pietrelcina, a Capuchin priest who bore the wounds of Christ's passion, was beatified in 1999, the liturgical celebrations honoring him were authorized for Italy and for the Franciscan family. When he was canonized in 2002, such celebrations were authorized for the whole world.

Our increasingly globalized and interconnected world makes this distinction difficult to maintain. A blessed such as Padre Pio, and later Mother Teresa of Calcutta (beatified in 2003), can already have a worldwide reputation for holiness.

Q: Why are some blesseds never canonized? Is there a formal waiting period between the two stages?

A: Unless someone is recognized as a martyr, a miracle is needed for beatification. Even for martyrs, a miracle is needed for canonization. There is usually a formal group promoting a person's canonization or beatification. There is no formal waiting period between beatification and canonization. As noted above, only three years passed between those two events for Padre Pio.

Q: What is the difference between All Saints Day and All Souls Day? When was each feast added to the liturgical calendar?

A: All Saints Day honors all the saints, especially those whose feast day is not observed worldwide and those not yet formally recognized as saints. In the *Dictionary of Catholic Devotions,* Michael Walsh says that this feast, begun in the fourth century, was first celebrated on May 13 and later moved to November 1.

On All Souls Day, we focus on those who are in purgatory. In sixth-century Spain, the Monday after Pentecost included special prayers for the dead. St. Odilo, abbot of Cluny (d. 1049), chose November 2 as the date to pray for deceased monks; the church later expanded this custom.

Q: What is the scriptural basis for praying for the dead in purgatory?

A: Belief in an afterlife is affirmed in the Hebrew Scriptures only in a few writings of the first and second centuries BC. In 2 Maccabees 12:38–46, Judas Maccabeus, leader of a Jewish revolt against the Syrians, orders sacrifices of atonement be offered for deceased Jewish soldiers who were discovered to have worn pagan amulets, or charms. In 1 Thessalonians 4:13–8, St. Paul tells the Christians that those who have died will rise when Christ returns in glory. Paul urges them to "console one another with these words." Praying for the deceased became part of that consolation.

| NOTES |

Introduction

1. Gordon Gilsdorf, *The Same Five Notes* (Francetown, N.H.: Golden Quill, 1967).
2. "A Saint," was originally published in his book of poetry, *The Color of Gratitude: And Other Spiritual Surprises* (Maryknoll, N.Y.: Orbis, 2009), p. 138.

Chapter Two

1. See http://www.beith-morounoye.org/library/Bibliography_Mor_Ephrem_Maronite.htm.
2. John Chrysostom, *In Evangelium S. Matthei,* hom. 50:3–4. pp. 58, 508–509. See www.vatican.va/edocs/ENG0821/p3.htm.

Chapter Four

1. Sister Roberta McKelvie, O.S.F., also contributed to this profile.
2. Sister Louanna Orth, S.N.D. de N., also contributed to this profile.
3. Mary-Cabrini Durkin also contributed to this profile.

Chapter Five

1. For more information about devotions, see *Selected Letters of Saint Jane Frances de Chantal.* (London: R & T Washbourne, 1918), p. 177.

Chapter Six

1. Thomas Merton, *Seeds of Contemplation* (Boston: Shambhala, 1961), p. 206.

Chapter Eight

1. Thérèse of Lisieux, *The Story of a Soul.* Thomas Taylor, trans. (New York: Cosimo, 1912), p. 69.
2. John Paul II, "Homily at Canonization of St. Padre Pio" www.ewtn.com/library/papaldoc/JP2PIOCN.HTM.

Chapter Eleven

1. John Neumann, *Declaration on Christian Education* (Huntington, Ind.: Our Sunday Visitor, 1966).

Chapter Twelve

1. Phyllis McGinley, *Saint-Watching* (New York: Crossroad, 1982), p. 3.
2. William James, *The Varieties of Religious Experience: A Study of Human Nature* (New York: Collier, 1961), p. 358.
3. Ronald Rolheiser, *Secularity and the Gospel: Being Missionaries to Our Children* (New York: Crossroad, 2006), p. 77.
4. Faustina Kowalska, *Diary of Saint Maria Faustina Kowalska: Divine Mercy in My Soul* (Stockbridge, Mass.: Marian, 2008), p. 281.

Frequently Asked Questions

1. Paul IV, "Decree on the Adaptation and Renewal of Religious Life," *Perfectae Caritatis,* www.vatican.va. October 28, 1965, #2.

BIBLIOGRAPHY AND RECOMMENDED READING

Allegri, Renzo. *Padre Pio: Man of Hope.* Cincinnati: Servant, 2000.

Bartoli, Marco. *Saint Clare: Beyond the Legend.* Cincinnati: St. Anthony Messenger Press, 2010.

Bodo, Murray. *Francis: The Journey and the Dream.* Cincinnati: St. Anthony Messenger Press, 1988.

Delio, Ilia. *Clare of Assisi: A Heart Full of Love.* Cincinnati: St. Anthony Messenger Press, 2007.

Ellsberg, Robert. *All Saints: Daily Reflections on Saints, Prophets, and Witnesses of our Time.* New York: Crossroad, 1997.

Fink, John F. *Married Saints.* Staten Island, N.Y.: Alba House, 1999.

Foley, Leonard, and Pat McCloskey. *Saint of the Day: Lives, Lessons and Feasts.* Cincinnati: St. Anthony Messenger Press, 2009.

Hill, Brennan. *Unlikely Spiritual Heroes.* Cincinnati: St. Anthony Messenger Press, 2010.

James, William. *The Varieties of Religious Experience: A Study of Human Nature.* New York: Collier, 1961.

John of the Cross and E. Allison Peers. *The Essential St. John of the Cross.* Radford, Va.: Wilder, 2008.

Kowalska, Faustina. *Diary of Saint Maria Faustina Kowalska: Divine Mercy in My Soul.* Stockbridge, Mass.: Marian, 2008.

Loehr, Gina. *The Four Teresas.* Cincinnati: Servant, 2010.

Marks, Patricia. *A Retreat With Edith Stein: Trusting God's Purpose.* St. Anthony Messenger Press, 2001.

Matura, Thaddée. *Francis of Assisi: Writer and Spiritual Master.* Cincinnati: St. Anthony Messenger Press, 2005.

McGinley, Phyllis. *Saint-Watching.* New York: Crossroad, 1982.

Neumann, John. *Declaration on Christian Education.* Huntington, Ind.: Our Sunday Visitor, 1966.

O'Neel, Brian. *39 New Saints You Should Know*. Cincinnati: Servant, 2010.

Rolheiser, Ronald. *Secularity and the Gospel: Being Missionaries to Our Children*. New York: Crossroad, 2006.

Tetlow, Joseph A. *Ignatius Loyola: Spiritual Exercises*. New York: Crossroad, 1992.

Thérèse of Lisieux and Robert J. Edmonson. *The Story of a Soul: St. Thérèse of Lisieux, a New Translation*. Brewster, Mass.: Paraclete, 2006.

Turpin, Joanne. *Twelve Apostolic Women*. Cincinnati: St. Anthony Messenger Press, 2004.

————. *Women in Church History: 21 Stories for 21 Centuries*. Cincinnati: St. Anthony Messenger Press, 2007.

Walsh, Michael J. *Dictionary of Catholic Devotions*. San Francisco: HarperSanFrancisco, 1993.

Woodward, Kenneth L. *Making Saints: How the Catholic Church Determines Who Becomes a Saint, Who Doesn't, and Why*. New York: Simon and Schuster, 1990.

| CONTRIBUTORS |

KATHY FINLEY is the author of several books including, *Savoring God: Praying With All Our Senses* (Ave Maria), *The Liturgy of Motherhood: Moments of Grace* (Sheed & Ward), *Welcome! Prayers for New and Pregnant Parents* (Liguori), *Amen! Prayers for Families With Children* (Liguori), and *Prayers for the Newly Married* (ACTA).

MITCH FINLEY is the author of more than thirty books, most recently *It's Not the Same Without You: Coming Home to the Catholic Church* (Doubleday), *101 Ways to Happiness: Nourishing Body, Mind and Soul* (Liguori), *Whispers of God's Love: Touching the Lives of Loved Ones After Death* (Liguori), and *Key Moments in Church History* (Sheed & Ward).

VICTORIA HÉBERT and DENIS SABOURIN, have collaborated, translated, and edited over twenty-five religious publications, primarily concentrating on the hagiographies of the saints. Currently living in Québec (Canada), happily retired—she from over fifteen years as religious magazine editor, he from his career as management consultant—they still dabble as freelance editors.

ALBERT HAASE, O.F.M., was ordained a Franciscan priest in 1983 and is a popular preacher, teacher, spiritual director, and radio personality. A former missionary to mainland China for over eleven years, he is the author of five books on popular spirituality. He is the director of the International Institute for Clergy Formation based at Seton Hall University, South Orange, N.J. He is also the cohost of "Spirit and Life," a radio show heard every weekend on the Relevant Radio Network, Baraga Broadcasting, and The Presence Radio Network.

JOAN MCKAMEY is the editor of *Everyday Catholic* and writes the "Seen and Heard" column for the monthly e-newsletter *Faith Formation Update*.

PAT MCCLOSKEY, O.F.M., is the former editor-in-chief of *St. Anthony Messenger* magazine and the author of its "Ask a Franciscan" column. He holds master's degrees in theology, divinity, and Franciscan studies. Author of six books and many articles, he has also revised and updated the bestselling titles *Believing in Jesus* and the last two editions of *Saint of the Day*. His most recent book is *Ask a Franciscan: Answers to Catholic Questions*.

ROBERT F. MORNEAU is currently the auxiliary bishop of the diocese of Green Bay and the author of several books and *Catholic Updates*.

FR. ANTHONY J. SALIM is pastor of St. Anthony of Padua, Cincinnati, Ohio, and has been involved in religious education for the past thirty years, lecturing widely in adult education programs, chiefly in Eastern Church studies and Scripture study. He has been a catechetical presenter at the USCCB Ecumenical and Interfaith Committee, and was appointed to the NCCB National Advisory Board for the National Directory for Catechesis, representing the Eastern Catholic Churches in the United States.

WILLIAM H. SHANNON is a priest of the diocese of Rochester, New York, and the founding president of the International Thomas Merton Society. He is professor emeritus in the religious studies department at Nazareth College. He is also the author of several *Catholic Updates* and books, including *Here on the Way to There: A Catholic Perspective on Dying and What Follows* (St. Anthony Messenger Press).

JOANNE TURPIN is the author of several books including *Twelve Apostolic Women* and *Women in Church History: 21 Stories for 21 Centuries* (St. Anthony Messenger Press).

MARY CUMMINS WLODARSKI is a contributor to St. Anthony Messenger Press and the coauthor (with Judith Dunlap) of the popular series *God Is Calling*.